Roof Gardens,
Balconies and Terraces

Roof
Gardens,
Balconies
and
Terraces

Photography by Jerry Harpur

Text by David Stevens

Rizzoli
NEW YORK

First published in the United States of America
in 1997 by
RIZZOLI INTERNATIONAL PUBLICATIONS, INC.
300 Park Avenue South, New York, NY 10010

First published in the United Kingdom in 1997 by
Mitchell Beazley, an imprint of Reed International
Books Limited, Michelin House, 81 Fulham Road,
London SW3 6RB

ISBN 0-8478-2015-7
LC 96-71420

Editors: Alex Bennion, Cathy Lowne, Diane Pengelly
Art Editor: Glen Wilkins
Designer: Sarah Davies
Production: Rachel Lynch
Artwork: David Ashby

Reproduction by Colourpath, London
Produced by Mandarin Offset
Printed and bound in China

Half title A carefully planned roof garden can increase immeasurably both your living space and your enjoyment of it.

Title page A roof garden has a drama all its own and gives you an opportunity to create a space entirely reflecting your personality.

Left The views from a terrace at ground level can be greatly enhanced by framing it, here with an arcade of softening plants.

Right Colour is a vital tool in garden design. Whether bold or muted, it should always be used coherently.

Contents

Introduction

To many people living in cities or towns, building a roof garden or redesigning an under-used balcony can be the only opportunity they will have to create a green oasis and an area of relative peace and privacy away from the urban bustle. Space is always at a premium in towns, so adding outside rooms to your home where you can sit, eat and entertain, or your children can play safely in the open air, is a wonderful means through which you can increase your living area. More than that, roof gardens and balconies have a major advantage over gardens that are at ground level: higher than many of the surrounding buildings, they can often provide beautiful and stunning views over day- and night-time cityscapes and these views can be exploited to form an integral part of the design of your garden.

Above left A warm colour scheme, vibrant planting and a distant glimpse of the landscape beyond all combine to create the ideal outdoor room, which can be sheltered, sunny and, above all, a private, restful haven.

Left Where views are important it is essential to invite them into your living space with a low boundary. If this is tempered with foliage, there will be a gradual transition between near and far.

Right Roofscapes are the stuff of aerial gardens – a kaleidoscope of windows, tiles and nearby balconies. A great joy of vernacular architecture is the sensitive use of traditional materials, something that modern designers should take heed of.

Above Comfortably furnished verandas provide the ultimate link between the inside and outside of your house, particularly in a hot climate where shade, combined with what breeze might be available, is often a necessity.

Above Exterior living space can be a vital addition to that inside the house. Here the link is reinforced in the colour scheme, paving materials and in the reflective quality of the pool.

Raised terraces are a perfect way of reworking the space in a garden at ground level. If there are areas that you feel are wasted, perhaps because they have too steep a slope to do anything except grass over them, a raised deck will provide a level platform on which you can create an entirely new part of the garden, with raised beds, seating, some plant-filled pots and perhaps a pond or a barbecue area. Like balconies and roof gardens, terraces can act as outside rooms, related to the inside of your home as much as to the rest of the garden. As such they may alter the way in which you use your garden: having somewhere pleasant to sit, eat or entertain will mean that you are able to spend more of your time out of doors.

In *Roof Gardens, Balconies and Terraces*, Jerry Harpur and I have set out with two specific aims. The first is to inspire you and to show you how some of the world's best garden designers have approached the unique problems of designing for the relatively small spaces occupied by roof gardens, balconies and terraces. Jerry has travelled across much of the world, including Italy, the United States, South America, the Netherlands, South and North Africa, Australia and Britain for the last year, tracking down and photographing many of the world's most beautiful and innovative roof gardens, balconies and terraces, each with its own character and style.

The book's aim is to provide guidance on all aspects of creating your own outdoor living space. The book is divided into five chapters: Design, Structure, Plants, Maintenance, and Accessories. Design focuses on what you may want from your garden, how to lay it out while making the best use of space and surroundings, and how to select an appropriate style. There is also an explanation of the basic rules of design, pattern, colour, size, texture and shape, as well as how to use them to manipulate the areas at your disposal.

Structure looks at the practical aspects of building a roof garden, balcony or terrace, including safety, structural and dimensional surveys, how to draw a scale plan, boundaries, flooring, where to place heavy beds and screens, and steps and overheads.

The chapter on plants shows you how to select plants that will suit the conditions in your garden and fulfil specific requirements such as focal points, screening, ground cover and colour. It gives clues both on how to arrange the plants in beds, pots and borders as well as on how to draw up a planting plan, so that the plants you buy not only form a coherent pattern but won't fall into the expensive mistakes category.

The section on maintenance offers advice on keeping both the hard landscape and the plants in the best condition possible. As well as stressing the importance of keeping the structural elements, boundaries, floors, screens and beds maintained and free of rot, rust and holes, I discuss the benefits of regular plant care – how often plants should be watered, how much food they should be given, how they should be trained, and when they should be pruned.

As accessories and ornaments are the most personal items in any garden, the final chapter simply gives advice on the different types avail-

Above The best gardens are an integral part of the architecture they adjoin. Arthur Erickson is a consummate designer and this composition is the perfect moulding of home, garden, mirror pool and the waters of Puget Sound in Washington State, USA.

able and how such items as statues, ponds and water features, urns, lighting, decorative trellis, *trompe-l'oeil* and garden furniture can best be used and positioned.

The greatest advantage of having a roof garden, balcony or terrace is that it will add an extra dimension to your home. It will be as much an outdoor extension of the inside of your home as it is a part of the garden. As well as providing extra space, all these additional areas are places for relaxation and enjoyment; you will find that eating breakfast on your balcony or roof garden on a Sunday morning can seem a world away from the usual weekday rush.

Design
in your mind's eye...

This is when you can really use your imagination. Spend a while considering how to use the new area of your garden. Reflect on the look and ambience that you want to create: modern, traditional, formal or informal. Think about plants, furniture, materials, tones and textures and how best to use them.

...and on paper

Repeat the process on paper. Visualize yourself and your family in it. Look at the areas of sun and shade, the views you want to exploit and those you need to hide. Move the screens, plants and furniture around until they feel right.

Left One of the most important design rules is that you should keep the layout as strong and simple as possible. Here, the strong line of the cacti forms a perfect border to the plain but beautiful terrace.

Planning the site

Design is a subtle business. Good design should combine strength of purpose, compatibility with the surroundings and, above all, simplicity. Overcomplication is the antithesis of good design and nowhere is this more apparent than in a garden. The vast array of materials, plants, containers and furniture in any garden centre, shop or nursery gives only a small idea of the kind of temptation facing the garden designer. A degree of self-control is essential if the space is not to become a jumble of unrelated objects. In many ways, the physical constraints of gardening above ground level can help, as they force the designer to begin with the essentials.

Design for your own needs

The whole subject of design is confusing to many people and suggests unattainable schemes in glossy magazines or coffee-table books. Nothing could be further from the truth: design is not just about fitting a particular scheme into a space; it is primarily about suiting and reflecting your own personality. You and your family or friends are the ones who will enjoy the space, and it is you who must determine how it is to be laid out. You should never copy exactly a scheme intended for a different garden; it may look fine where it is, but will, without doubt, prove unworkable for you.

Starting from scratch

The exact position and size of a roof garden or balcony is usually predetermined by the space already available. Occasionally, however, you can build a new balcony, or vertically extend a house so that there is fresh potential for living space outside. In such instances it makes good sense to work with the architect from the start. Explain to him or her what you want from the area, so that any favourable aspects, shelter and views can all be taken into account at the planning stage. The structural survey would then include the appropriate information and the building work would make provision for access and services such as electricity and water. There may be several areas and exit points that have potential, so ensure that both you and your designer take all these into account. Such an approach is far better – and inevitably cheaper – than trying to add the garden at a later date.

Above left Plants play a major role in any garden, but on a roof or balcony have a special function in softening austere surroundings. Strong foliage plants, like hostas, are ideal for this purpose.

Left Even the smallest balcony can provide room to sit and relax. Folding chairs save space, planting brings flowers and fragrance, while the sculpture echoes the line of London's Tower Bridge.

Right Simplicity of design is usually the key to tiny gardens and here the neatly-tiled floor is echoed in the squared trellis and white parasol. Burgeoning pots prevent any austerity and naturally lead you through the open area.

Above There should be a positive transition between inside and outside. Here the paving pattern encourages the eye to run down the garden to the simple planting screen.

Above Even the smallest and most uncompromising shape can provide room for sitting and dining if it is handled with flair. Continuity is achieved by the vertical boarding and handrail, while the backdrop of trees provides a green envelope.

Design constraints

The load-bearing potential of a roof or balcony will determine where beds, containers and other heavy features can be safely placed. The climate and aspect will dictate what provision is needed for shelter from winds or hot sun. High-level decks fall into much the same structural category as roof gardens and you should consult a specialist designer, architect or engineer.

A word of warning: few architects specialize in roof garden design, so choose your designer carefully, on recommendation if possible. Check the company has the necessary experience in specialized building codes, as well as what it takes to get the best out of the structure and available space.

Raised terraces or decks at ground level are a different matter, as there are fewer limits on space and weight, and there may be considerable scope for variation in where you put them as well as greater freedom in the choice of materials (see pages 40–43). Take your time over a basic survey that includes views, shelter, prevailing winds and the track of the sun throughout the day, both in summer and in winter.

In hot climates, potential terrace and sitting areas may virtually surround the house, allowing you to choose between sun and shade as the sun moves round during the day. Verandas are particularly successful in this regard. Terraces need not touch the building and it is often possible to put them in other parts of the garden where they can take on quite a different and perhaps more informal character. As always, they will need to be planned and sited carefully as they will almost certainly become major focal points within the overall composition and linkage with other parts of the garden will need to be taken into account.

On a roof, balcony or terrace there are often constraints of size and location and this basic planning process is important to ensure that you

Right Style is always difficult to define, but should always reflect the personality of the owner. This terrace is a cool, lush and relaxed refuge that relies on the careful use of natural materials and impeccable planting for its success.

do not make any expensive mistakes. At the start of all planning work you should assess what space you have and then plan into it everything you might need (how to carry out a structural and dimensional survey is covered on pages 52–58). Preparing a detailed plan will enable you to plot accurately both the dimensions of the area and all the factors that act upon it, including its orientation to the sun, good and poor views, prevailing winds, changes of level, access points, surrounding walls or roofs, available services, and existing floor coverings or other structures. Together these factors will determine not only just how the space is laid out but also the style of the garden.

One great advantage of preparing a design is that nothing is cast in stone. You can change your mind as often as you like, roughing out different ideas, trying different permutations and firming things up in order to progress towards a garden that is uniquely suitable to you and your needs. In other words, the first scheme you prepare should certainly not be the last; it is worth taking the time to rough out ideas as there may be different, but equally acceptable, solutions to any specific design problem.

What does the rest of the family want?

Bear in mind that as the garden is to be used by several people or a family, it is important to also listen to the other users' ideas. Elitist design that ignores the real function of a garden is usually sterile, so be open to suggestions.

Preparing the design

Initially, you should just rough out what you want to place where, whether it be sitting space, a dining or play area or features such as raised beds or water. At this stage it is immaterial whether the

PLANNING THE SITE
The finished garden scheme is drawn out to scale, taking into account the information gathered earlier.

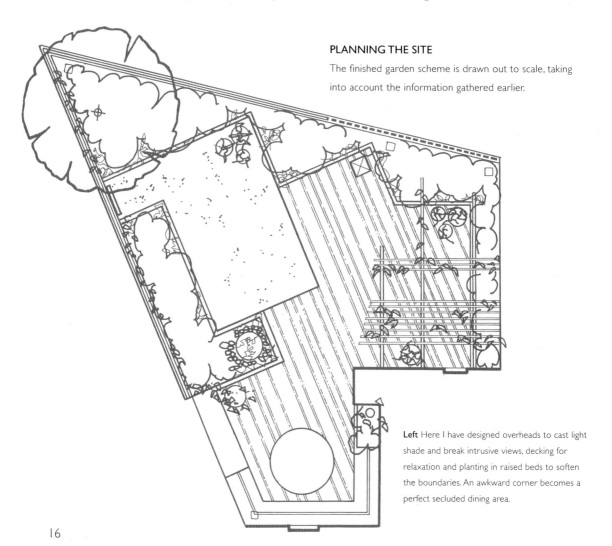

Left Here I have designed overheads to cast light shade and break intrusive views, decking for relaxation and planting in raised beds to soften the boundaries. An awkward corner becomes a perfect secluded dining area.

size of the area is large or small or at roof or ground level, although a small space will inevitably need to be thought about in simpler terms to avoid it looking crowded.

The importance of preparing a scale drawing of the area is clear: it allows you to see the exact proportions of everything and the space available for the various features. Make plenty of copies of the plan: this allows you to try different permutations, shifting the components about and seeing how they relate to each other. Some people make a simple model as this allows them to see the composition in three dimensions rather than two. Alternatively, if you want to see how things work out at full size, the area itself can be pegged or marked out with the shapes and the space simply divided with makeshift screens.

These techniques will allow you to visualize different ideas without actually undertaking any

Above Changes in level and direction can offer the opportunity to create separate garden rooms, naturally generating movement from one place to another. Planting can partially hide a view, allowing you to wonder what lies around the corner.

construction work. When you eventually arrive at a final layout you can prepare the design itself by filling in the detail, choosing materials and working out the pattern that best suits the shape of the area and is appropriate to the adjoining building or surroundings.

The design can then either act as the basis for a do-it-yourself project, be passed to one or more contractors for detailed quotations or act as your briefing document for a garden designer or architect. Whatever the final outcome, the exercise will allow you to gain a far better idea of how you will use the areas involved and be the basis for a fuller enjoyment of the finished garden.

Style considerations

A garden that lacks sympathy with the building it adjoins and with its environs rarely looks or works at its best. Good architects and designers create spaces that respect and are compatible with their surroundings. A problem often arises with the popularity of a style, whether it be 'cottage', 'formal', 'Japanese' or something else. While any of these may be appropriate, and indeed superb in the right setting, they can simply be a fashionable cliché in others. The incongruity of a traditional cottage garden adjoining a crisp contemporary façade would diminish the inherent charms of both house and garden. As a rule, a clean, modern composition will suit a newer building while something more traditional might be successful adjoining a period house.

Linking inside and out

Many people see the spaces inside and outside as two separate entities, when they should be linked as strongly as possible and carry on to use their immediate surroundings and more distant views to their advantage. In this way you can achieve a progression from inside to outside and beyond, drawing together materials, colour schemes, furnishing and plants into an all-embracing whole that will help to create a feeling of space at any point in the overall composition.

Doorways

Where doors give immediate access, the transition from inside to outside is often straightforward, but it can prove more difficult in the case of a roof garden, where narrow stairs or even ladders are more usual. Such a break in continuity makes it difficult to create a natural linkage and it

Above left The best rooms, whether inside or out, invariably have fine views, and this should work both from the house into the garden and from the garden towards the building.

Left Creating a successful living space has much to do with choice of compatible materials. Here floor tiles are complemented by the warm-coloured walls, vernacular buttress and traditional coping.

Above The organization of a formal space need not necessarily be rigid and in this case the centrally framed table is perfectly offset by the clipped balls that in turn frame the view.

may be worth considering how to improve it, both to facilitate access (especially while the building work is going on) and to allow a smooth visual transition from inside to out.

Having said that, there is an obvious and pleasing drama in climbing a well-constructed spiral staircase from one space to another, especially if this linkage is also themed with plants and compatible colour. Try to make the most of your

Above Steps are always an invitation to enter a garden. Here they have been further enhanced by simple planting in pots and by the plant-clad wall, which has been colour-washed to tone in with the doors and shutters.

Above These broad and generous steps are perfectly complemented by the introduction of the rounded domes of foliage that soften what might otherwise be an austere modern composition of shades of grey and geometric forms.

LINKING INSIDE AND OUT

The linkage between a house and the immediate area outside should be as seamless as possible.

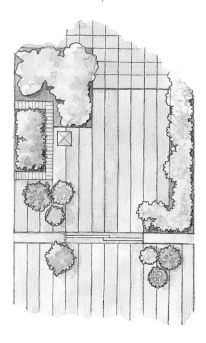

Above The continuation of the decking patterns and planting either side of the glass doors smooths the transition from one to the other.

access points, using them to tie your interior and exterior spaces together.

The ideal is to have large areas of glass dividing inside and out, creating minimal visual disruption. Pots and containers can be grouped on both sides, disguising the dividing line.

Flooring

Just as doorways and how they are treated are important, so too are flooring materials. Here is an obvious opportunity to link inside and out by allowing similar surfaces to run together. A timber floor inside can be a cue for decking outside; tiles can relate to tiles; certain kinds of paving can look superb on both sides of a glass divide; while even more complex designs might involve the flow of water, lighting and planting from interior to exterior living space. When working out a pattern, try to make sure that modules, shapes or lines run continuously from inside to out. Paving or boards should be aligned rather than offset, with minimal visual disruption (*see above right*).

Ceilings and overheads

Although we tend to look down more often than up, the ceiling can be used as an additional link. The lines of a timber ceiling or beams can be echoed by overheads outside. This effect could be enhanced by installing subtle lighting strips on either side of the divide.

Shade and tone

Colour, often undervalued and underused, is another theme that can draw house and garden together. If you have a decorative scheme inside and an adjoining wall outside, why not paint the outside wall in the same shade? Awnings offer an ideal opportunity to pick up a fabric pattern from an interior scheme. Incidental features such as pots, containers and furniture can be chosen in much the same way, with a coherent and simple theme in mind.

Above Such a complicated, but beautifully detailed floor pattern, needs perfectly conceived geometry, immaculate construction and just the right setting to look at its best.

Below Overhead beams can provide the perfect link between inside and out, casting dappled shade, blocking a view from neighbouring windows and providing a frame for climbing plants.

Dividing the space

Roof gardens, balconies and raised terraces are generally far smaller than entire gardens at ground level. This means that they can be thought about and planned in much the same way as rooms inside the house and many elements can be addressed using the same techniques. Unlike their larger counterparts at ground level, roof gardens, balconies and raised terraces can be compared even further with rooms by the simple fact that they have floors, are partially or completely walled and may well have a ceiling in the form of overheads, beams or a canopy. Few people would think of simply scattering furniture, carpets, paintings or other features at random around a room inside the home, yet this so often occurs with furniture, ornaments, beds and pots outside. While we are conditioned to think about planning and allocating space in living areas, bedrooms and kitchens, I feel it is a great pity that those same perfectly valid rules are seldom applied to gardens.

Above left The subtle division of space is one of a garden designer's most valuable tools, providing the vital ingredients of tension, mystery and surprise. Just what those divisions are, and where they are positioned, will depend upon the individual setting.

Left Dividers need not be permanent structures, and moveable objects such as pots and furniture can effectively guide you through a space and create separate areas or rooms.

Above Dividing walls and an arch smothered with climbing roses invite you up the steps and into the partially hidden, more distant garden. The view is terminated by the central urn and there is a delightful transition between sunlight and shade.

What goes where?

The initial job, before choosing materials or creating a pattern, is to allocate space and to position the garden elements. This can be carried out roughly on copies of a scale drawing of the area. Look at your survey and identify the basic constraints and advantages of the site. What is the prevailing wind direction and does the wind need breaking or filtering in some way? Where does the sun track throughout the day and which are the shady areas? Your answers may suggest specific areas suitable for sitting, dining and entertaining. Just where are the good or poor views? They may need emphasis or they may need to be screened. Are you overlooked by a neighbour's window? A carefully positioned small tree in a container or the addition of overhead beams could improve your privacy. Are there any changes in level and,

if so, are they dramatic enough to necessitate steps or a ramp? Changes in level could perhaps be emphasized by a water feature, raised bed or carefully positioned focal point. Where are the doors and windows? You could use the former as the starting point for a main garden axis, and position a special feature within view of the latter to provide year-round interest from indoors.

Practical points

Most gardens have to serve practical functions as well as contain purely decorative elements: roofs and balconies are no different from their cousins on the ground in this respect. There is something immensely satisfying and visually pleasing about a string of brightly coloured washing, for example, which shows that your home belongs to real people rather than in a glossy magazine. Many a roof garden would benefit from a compost bin for trimmings and leaves (the resultant product would provide good plant nutrition), or there may be room for play equipment, a sand box or a well-designed storage area for toys.

On the plan, these features can be shown in an approximate position; there is little need for detailed design at this stage. The important thing is to position the various elements of the garden reasonably accurately.

Tension, mystery and surprise

These three elements are the key to creating a worthwhile garden design regardless of scale, whether it is a rolling landscape or the smallest balcony. Any space that can be seen at a single glance is far less interesting than one divided into different areas that can be discovered as you move through it. Obviously, in a small area there is less space available to create a number of different divisions, but a simple screen, a low planter or bench can still act as a divider on a roof garden or balcony and create greater interest.

If you have enough room, it can be delightful to allocate different purposes to different areas: a dining space, a play corner or an area for sitting, entertaining or barbecuing. If these areas are linked to their counterparts indoors, the whole design will be more coherent visually.

When each space has its own theme or purpose, the visitor tends to remain for a given length of time in each area, making the garden feel larger than its true size.

Screens

The way in which you divide the area will be determined by the surroundings; for example, high dividers or screens may be necessary in order to keep a particular area private, but low ones will be sufficient to create 'rooms'. Screens can be constructed to above eye-level and smothered with planting, or some areas can be defined by built-in seating at a lower level. Higher planting could involve trees and shrubs, while arches and overheads can all play a part. A combination of these features might be used, one linking with

Left Screens can be one of the most effective dividers, providing an excellent windbreak and ideal frame for climbing plants. Such a complex design benefits from the tempering effect of foliage.

Above As a general rule too many styles and materials make a garden look too 'busy', but here the design of the various screens and fences becomes all the more effective by echoing that of the surrounding architecture.

CREATING TENSION AND MYSTERY

The positioning of gaps in a screen is of great importance, as it can dictate how people walk through the space.

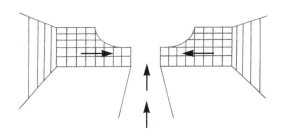

Above A narrow opening between two wings of trellis, hedging or other dividing material inevitably creates a feeling of tension and surprise for anyone walking through.

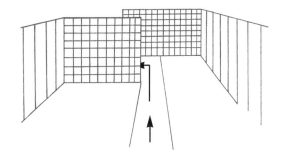

Above Where a path disappears from view there is always that question of mystery: just what does lie around the corner?

another and creating an overall subdivision of space at different points of the composition.

Dividers need not be above eye-level to be effective. Because your line of sight is lower when you are seated, even if you can see over a screen, it still defines spaces, giving it its own character.

Where you position the gaps in screens is important. Tension is created and increased as

Left Focal points always need careful positioning as they are purposeful eye-catchers. Remember that strong colour not only provides added vibrancy but brings a focal point towards you.

Below Too much white in a garden can lead to glare, but here it is tempered by the pastel furniture, planting and medium height raised bed that softens the higher wall.

you move towards an arch or a gap in a screen; as you move between the wings it is at its greatest, but releases with a surprise as you enter the new 'room' beyond to be greeted with a quite different theme or view. Mystery – just what lies beyond a wing of planting or a screen – is perhaps the most delightful element of garden design (*see p.25*).

Even on a balcony, particularly a long one, a short screen or subdivision can make the overall shape more attractive and manageable. Such dividers could be staggered along the balcony so that you zig-zag through the area (*see opposite page, above right*). This is a favourite trick of garden designers as it makes you walk slightly farther, thereby increasing the sense of space.

Focal points

Features such as water, statuary and urns can be used to draw the eye and form important focal points in the overall composition. Think about them in some detail when you are preparing the main design as they can provide directional emphasis, leading the eye across a roof. They can also be the focus of a vista on a long balcony or provide the sight and sound of water on a split-level terrace. Although some features may be occasionally moved or adjusted, many will form permanent or semi-permanent parts of the design. However, as the punctuation marks of the garden, they should always be used sparingly.

If you are concerned about the weight of an ornamental feature, return to your initial survey, check which parts of the roof or balcony are strong enough, and position the item accordingly. The best areas will normally be around the perimeter, or where a load-bearing member provides strength beneath the surface.

Right Steps will naturally lead the eye upward, and if the view can be terminated in some way then drama ensues. This fine urn gains greater importance by being placed on a plinth at the top of the flight of steps, to which your eye is led by the darker stripe of the brick path. The walls are simply constructed from well laid, pointed concrete blocks that provide a no-nonsense foil to the planting that tumbles over the edges.

Pattern and shape

Gardens come in all shapes and sizes and the patterns in which the various elements of the different areas are laid out have an enormous impact on how the space works in both visual and practical terms.

An obvious parallel can be drawn between how decorative effects are used indoors and how they are used on roof gardens, balconies and terraces. For example, indoors, wallpaper with a large, bold pattern tends to emphasize a surface, drawing the eye towards it and making the room feel smaller. On the other hand, a delicate, small-scale pattern, or a sponged or rag-rolled finish, tends to create a feeling of greater space. The same principle works in the garden, where a fence or screen of wide boards will seem closer than a fence or screen of narrow slats or a light trellis. The way in which you choose and use plants follows the same general rule: large, bold leaves will draw the boundary in, fine feathery shapes will push it out. The elements of your garden can be selected and positioned in order to manipulate the space visually.

Overheads

Heavy, large-section overheads seem to compress vertical space, while narrower and lighter timbers have an airy feel and are thus less oppressive. The same principle applies to the shadows that they cast onto the floor: thin, light shadow patterns will break the visual weight of a large expanse of paving as does sunlight that is filtered through the small-scale foliage of a tree such as silver birch or mountain ash.

Flooring

As well as the surface patterns and textures you choose, the way in which you lay or arrange the flooring materials has a bearing on apparent space, as strong lines tend to draw the eye in a particular direction. Long boards, laid so that they run away from a doorway or main viewing point, will tend to accelerate the view towards an imaginary vanishing point. As your eye travels

MOVEMENT THROUGH NARROW SPACES

In a long, narrow garden, entered at one end, dividers can be positioned to make the area seem shorter and wider.

Above A floor of just a single paving material can become bland or a little too 'heavy', but when teamed with another contrasting surface the end result is far more interesting. Keep things simple though, as three materials would distract from the simplicity.

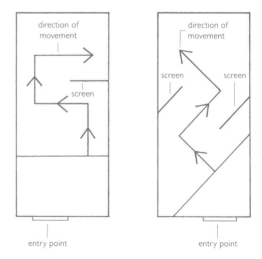

Above By taking a path up and across a garden, between screens or wings of planting, you introduce not only tension and surprise, but also force people to cover a greater distance.

Right Design continuity in this long, narrow balcony is achieved by matching the tone of the floor tiles with that of the old brick walls. Furniture also helps to dovide the area, although natural timber is far easier on the eye than painted furniture.

Above Any garden built up from strong flowing curves has a natural feeling of space and movement. In a reduced area, small modules on the floor, such as cobbles, can be laid up to the hedge and pool without cutting, and have no lines to distract from the main curves.

Left A rich paving pattern has much the same effect as a well-worked carpet inside the home, bringing scale and intimacy. Herringbone brick paving is both mellow and traditional.

along the uninterrupted shadow lines or joints, you tend to miss much of the detail along the way and the area might appear smaller. If, conversely, boards are laid across a view they will tend to slow the eye down and it will take longer to cross the area, so the space seems larger.

Broad deck boards will produce a more static visual effect than narrow ones will. I often vary board widths on a deck as I find that this can set up fascinating rhythms.

The scale of the paving or decking used also affects the perceived space. Small modules look and feel lighter than large ones, so the former should be used in an area where you want to maximize a feeling of space.

Most paving and hard landscape materials – boards, bricks, railway sleepers (ties), granite setts, wooden blocks or cobbles – can be laid to give directional emphasis, allowing you to manipulate the spaces at your disposal, and decking patterns can be arranged to lead the eye and help to disguise or emphasize the shapes around them.

Materials

You should also consider the number of different materials that are used in the garden. Remember that the old maxim 'less is more' makes good sense, particularly in small spaces where a busy pattern becomes obvious and obtrusive.

Using just a single boundary detail and one paving type will help to maximize the apparent space in a small area. In a larger garden there may be scope to increase the number of materials, but this should be done carefully, respecting the overall division of space, so that different treatments are found in the different 'rooms'.

This simplicity should run though all the main garden elements. When choosing additional furniture, pots, containers and statuary, try also to work to an overall theme in much the same way that you would when furnishing a room. Shape and pattern are infinitely variable tools, providing space and movement that can transform your outside living space.

Mind the gap

One further point is of great importance to the creation of any pattern. When drawing a scheme on paper, do not look in isolation at the shapes you are creating, but also consider the spaces that are left over; if you are not careful with the way you plant them or relate them to one another, the result can look uncomfortable or a mess of unrelated shapes. You should therefore think about the pattern of the area as a unified whole and not just about its most obvious parts.

Above Granite setts, or other small scale paving materials, can be laid to complex patterns, but attention to detail in both design and construction is absolutely vital because it will be very obvious if anything is misaligned.

Above Timber decking is an easily worked surface and can be cut and laid to an infinite number of patterns. As with any other paved surface, the pattern of the flooring should be kept as simple as possible; it will then add to the interest of the space rather than overwhelming the rest of it.

Manipulating shapes

The next thing for you to consider is the shape of the area with which you are dealing and how it can be used and manipulated visually to achieve its maximum potential. A designer's 'tricks of the trade' are simple devices that can be learned by anyone. The first rule is that the shape of a space generates movement in a particular direction: a long narrow garden, whether at ground level or in the air, will lead the eye down its space; a dog-legged area encourages you around the corner, and a square garden is static, at least within the confines of its boundaries.

Solutions for shapes

The key to most successful designs lies in being able to manipulate how people look at the area in question in order to get the best from it. You can use all of the elements of your garden to do this: the plants, dividers, focal points, features and floor patterns.

Long, narrow areas

In a long narrow space, laying a deck or paving pattern down its length and emphasizing the pattern by placing pots or seating down either side will make the garden look even longer and narrower as the eye rushes from one end to the other. In this case, the garden should be subdivided into a number of different areas, each with a different theme or purpose. If the spaces are large enough, this idea could be reinforced by giving each area different floor and boundary treatments. Such an approach will conceal the overall shape of the garden and superimpose a new and more visually manageable pattern.

The effect can be further enhanced through the way in which people are compelled to move through the space. If you are allowed to walk in a straight line from 'room' to 'room', the journey is a relatively fast one. If, however, the entry and exit points are staggered, it will take longer to negotiate the garden and the distance covered will be greater, thus increasing the apparent size of the garden.

The best design solutions to a garden of this shape will differ slightly depending on the exact position of the main view across and entry point

Above left Shapes, whether in two or three dimensions, have a positive role in how we perceive space. Here a contrasting paving leads the eye positively down and across the area.

Left Humour is an integral part of any design medium and mock wind socks on a roof make the sculptural point perfectly. They also check the view, before it moves on to the cathedral dome.

Right When you enter a long narrow roof or balcony from one end, the view opens up in front of you. To prevent the eye running straight to the opposite end, the area will need subdividing with points of interest to create more manageable spaces.

Above This self-contained dining area is framed by planting set at different heights in containers to either side, thus helping to disguise the long, narrow shape of the overall area.

Above Boards, bricks or any other surface laid across, rather than down a space, will emphasize the width and help draw the area apart. This can be reinforced by planting to create additional side-to-side movement as you walk through the garden.

into the garden. If you enter at one end of the area the space will stretch away from you, whereas if you approach the garden from the side there will be a shorter distance between you and the opposite boundary and the space will lead you away to either side.

In the second instance, if a major focal point is positioned exactly opposite the entry point, it tends to draw the eye immediately and make the short dimension seem even shorter. In a garden with the main view across the short axis, you should put a focal point to either side (*see below right*), at the edge of your vision, either from your viewpoint inside the house or from the main access into the garden. This will lead your eye away from the near point opposite toward the focal points that are farther away.

Angled areas

In a dog-leg garden, where the space either leads around the corner, or from area to area around a roof, there is obvious potential for floor, boundary and screening treatments to encourage you through the space. Flooring can be laid to echo a right-angled turn, so that your feet and eyes naturally follow the pattern. You will find that planting can be effective, with a sweep of vegetation that not only softens hard angles but leads you around the corner.

PLACING FOCAL POINTS

By using simple visual tricks, basic design rules can be used to manipulate space in any way that you wish.

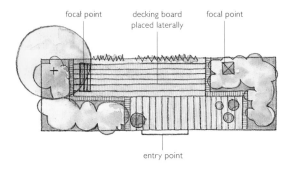

focal point   decking board placed laterally   focal point

entry point

Above If you enter a long narrow space from the centre, focal points to either side will draw the eye away from the shorter dimension ahead. An additional way of softening the focal points is by the use of carefully-chosen plants.

The vertical space could be defined by overheads developed to form a pergola (as attractive on a roof as at ground level), provided that there is adequate space. Pergolas have enormous drawing power, containing the key design elements of tension, mystery and surprise.

The route that a pergola follows need not be simply in a straight line: it can pass through an angle or a series of angles, and is therefore an especially invaluable tool in reinforcing the basic pattern of the garden.

One of a pergola's functions is to engender expectancy: it creates tension as you enter at one end, with tantalizing views to either side as you move through it, and an enormous release of energy as you emerge from the far end. For this reason, it must have somewhere positive to go. A pergola is a device for movement and if a journey through it ends in anti-climax or, worse, at a bad view, then the feature is degraded.

Above Angularity in a design provides positive movement and, in the right setting, acts as a link with adjoining architecture. Minimal planting emphasizes rather than detracts from the overall pattern.

Below Diagonals, even though geometric, can offer a more gentle progression through an area. Here the underlying pattern has been emphasized by the raised beds and edging.

Square areas

Square gardens are the most difficult from the designer's point of view, as they lack any positive directional movement. There are a number of solutions to this problem. One is to employ a pattern that uses diagonals: a line that runs between opposite corners is longer than one going from side to side or top to bottom, so using a design that incorporates this principle makes the garden look larger than it is, and the eye is distracted from the underlying static shape (*see below*).

Many people avoid incorporating right-angles in the garden, fearing that it will become far too static and 'hard'. However, a series of overlapping rectangles, perhaps at different heights and using a variety of materials, softened and punctuated by planting, can form a fascinating backdrop that can be linked positively into the geometry and architecture of the immediate surroundings.

Curves have the potential to provide an enormous sense of movement but are often poorly conceived and fussy rather than vigorous. To avoid this, curves should be based on positive radii that are worked out on the drawing board.

CREATING MOVEMENT IN A SQUARE SPACE

The entire shape of this square area is negated by the strong diagonals of the decking and beds.

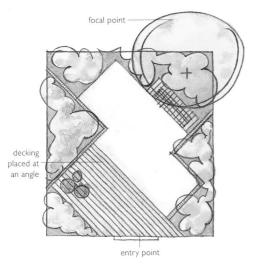

focal point

decking placed at an angle

entry point

Left Even in a comparatively small area you can create both space and movement by turning through an area. Decking is ideally suited to a change in direction and the eye is naturally led to the focal point formed by the urn.

Above Modern design is often based on a series of overlapping rectangles, based on an underlying grid. The resulting shapes can be given over to a combination of paving, planting, furniture and other incidental features.

Above A complex pattern such as this concentrates interest within the space, detracting from the surroundings. If you are faced with uncompromising boundaries or views which you wish to ignore, this can be a useful design tool.

Shapes based on a circle or a series of curves can form an effective disguise for a rectangular area. Most types of surfacing can be laid in a circular pattern and although it is difficult to shape raised beds to an exact curve it is not impossible, particularly if the roof is strong enough to carry brickwork. There is potential for manipulating such materials as artificial turf, gravels, stone chippings and glass beads, and circular shapes can also be echoed in arrangements of pots and containers.

Using your surroundings

On a roof garden you may have the wonderful addition of a fine view. This can be invaluable in drawing the eye out into a roof- or cityscape, which in turn lends itself to your composition. As such views are an integral part of the garden, you should encourage them in.

Framing the view

There is another design trick involved in the way that you go about framing the view, and it brings us back to the adage that 'less is more'. When I visit a garden with a fine view, either at ground level or on the roof, the clients often suggest that I should leave it exactly as it is. However, I think of a view in the same way as I would a good watercolour painting. This may look beautiful on a sheet of paper, but if you place it behind a mount it becomes sharper; if you select the perfect frame, although it is the same painting, your perception of it is immediately enhanced. In the garden we should think of framing the view, or several views, in some way.

A wide open view is often too expansive: too much to take in at one glance and therefore too dominant and all-encompassing. To 'improve' it you could, for example, blot out a less attractive area, perhaps bring in planting to one side and a screen to the other side, and finally use an overhead to define the upper limit.

Left Many fine views can be overpowering, but by partially hiding or framing them – perhaps with a wall and overhanging planting – you can make them even more effective.

There are infinite permutations, but the principle remains the same: if you heighten the drama and focus the view, you will have a powerful tool at your disposal. In this way you can 'borrow' a distant scene by drawing it into your space and keeping attention away from closer elements. You can also use the floor and boundary treatments as part of the focusing equipment. A board pattern can draw the eye towards a vista.

Above Containing a roof garden or balcony with planting not only acts as a safety measure but also softens the inevitable hard edges created by walls, fences and railings. In addition, the plants will bring colour, texture and interest to the composition.

Right A delicate, yet strong, boundary allows easy access to a view, framed by bars, that includes the island of Alcatraz. *Kniphofia* emphasizes the strong verticality of the pattern, its strong colour momentarily holding the eye within the garden.

Terraces: a wider choice

While the choice of materials is necessarily limited on balconies and roof gardens, because of space and weight constraints, a much wider selection is available for use on terraces at ground level. Suitable materials include stone of all kinds, pre-cast concrete, brushed aggregates, timber in the form of decking or railway sleepers (ties), gravel, wood or stone chippings, bricks and blocks. Avoid including a number of different surfaces: the point is to be selective, and while a single surface can seem bland or 'heavy', more than two may look too busy. Because one surfaces invariably lightens and balances another, two contrasting surfaces usually work well together.

Above left Containers not only offer endless opportunities for planting, they are also an integral part of the design, providing both division and focal points.

Left With their subtle shadow patterns, planting and surrounding screens can combine with decking and containers to form the basis for an ideal outdoor living space.

Above Steps should always be as broad and generous as possible, providing a gentle transition between different levels and tying terraced areas together in a positive way.

Right Pots are an ideal way of providing instant colour. In the form of bulbs and annual planting they can be changed from season to season and moved about the terrace at will, thereby altering the visual character of an area.

40

Materials, patterns and forms

Generally, areas near a building should be laid out in a crisp, 'architectural' manner in material that forms a natural link with the building. In this way a brick or stone house might suggest the use of brick or stone in the immediate terrace, while brushed aggregate or decking might be suitable near a contemporary concrete or timber building.

Paving

The way in which different paving materials are combined will depend to an extent on the basic pattern of the garden. This should be an extension of the building lines in order to help to link the house and garden together. You might have courses, or a grid, of brickwork that runs out from the building and is infilled with a contrasting material such as pre-cast concrete slabs, stone or brushed aggregate. Part of the pattern could consist of raised beds, planting at ground level, water, steps and built-in seating, all of which can be tied into the main modular pattern.

Many people like broken or 'crazy' paving, but the conflicting lines may clash with a cleaner

Left Colour need not be restricted to planting alone, although planting can help to tone down a vibrant floor that might otherwise dominate the situation.

Below Strength of purpose in architecture can often be successfully offset by equally strong terracing around the house, the one linking positively into the other.

façade. The answer here is to contain the paving within a contrasting grid or pattern that will help to stabilize the inherently busy surface.

Curves

Curves set close to a building need to be handled carefully if they are not to feel uncomfortable, but they can look superb if they are used in a positive way, with strong radii that link back to the underlying grid or building.

Terraces farther away from the house can be much more fluid in outline, echoing the possible informality of the garden at this point. Small modules or fluid materials, such as brick, granite setts, cobbles, wood chips or gravel, will conform to a curve without needing to be cut. Larger modules such as concrete slabs may need to be cut and this can be an expensive, time-consuming, noisy and difficult operation.

Overheads

In terraces as well as roof gardens, overheads and beams can form a particularly strong and attractive link with the building, extending the architectural lines into the garden and landscape.

Above Water in the natural landscape rarely runs in straight lines, but a curving pool, which in this case doubles as an occasional seat, has a natural feel.

Below One of the great advantages of small pots and containers in the garden is that they can easily be moved about to where they are needed at a particular time. Here they are disguising the hard right-angle formed by the larger planter.

Balconies

Balconies are in effect small roof gardens, and the same design guidelines apply, especially those concerning long, narrow spaces (see pages 33–34), as most balconies tend towards this shape. Their relatively small size means that designs should be kept as simple as possible: anything too 'busy' will be overpowering. The transition from inside to outside is usually uncomplicated, with no great changes in level, and so they can be linked easily through the use of pattern, materials, shade and tone. Balconies make ideal outdoor rooms.

Materials and features

Because the load-bearing potential of a balcony is limited, keep everything as light as possible and avoid grouping heavy items in one place. Also, because the space available is small, you will not have room for large numbers of pots and should keep special features to a minimum.

Flooring

Floors are usually straightforward, as they are already paved. It may be possible to resurface the floor, provided that the structure will accept the extra weight, and here there may be an opportunity to use a similar surface to that inside, perhaps sawn stone or tiles of some kind.

Screens and planters

One of the great charms of a balcony is the feeling of almost floating in space, but shelter and privacy are often at a premium. Screens, set to one or both sides can often help, with the style, shade and tone of these designed to reflect the

Above left Hanging gardens, such as these baskets, will naturally clothe vertical space. However, the containers will need to be securely fixed and regularly fed and watered to ensure that the plants are kept as healthy as possible.

Left Virtually every inch of space on this railing has been smothered with pot-grown plants. Although this arrangement will entail a high degree of maintenance, the end result will be worth the effort.

Above A decked balcony can dramatically increase your amount of living space. Not only will the railings act as a host to climbing plants but such a space is wonderfully light and airy.

building. Planters can often be built as a unit with the screens and, if set at either end of the balcony, they allow maximum space in the central areas for sitting and relaxation.

On a balcony that is both long enough to span the entire face of a building and accessible from a number of points, there may be an opportunity to subdivide the space with wings of trellis or screens. These can provide the key design elements of tension, mystery and surprise as you move through the space.

Awnings

Awnings on balconies, as on the roof, can cast soft swathes of shade but as wind may be a problem, they should be retractable. Fabric awnings can be used to extend the interior decorative scheme to the outside.

Using vertical space

On balconies, with their relatively limited floor space, explore the possibilities of hanging pots or planters on the walls, internal screens or railings. Planters could be built as an integral part of the railings, possibly with seating or other features. As with anything above ground level, all pots and planters must be securely fixed.

Above This simple paint scheme has the effect of unifying house and balcony, while the overheads set up fascinating patterns that will change throughout the day.

Above Most boundary structures, particularly those found on balconies, provide the ideal framework for all kinds of plants, especially climbers. The plants in turn help to reinforce the line of the underlying architecture.

Left The idea that a design should be kept as simple as possible applies equally to traditional or modern designs. In this case, the centrally placed pots add immeasurably to a classical composition.

Colour

While colour is usually understood and used with great sensitivity inside the home, the rules for using it are often forgotten or ignored outside. There are, obviously, a number of ways in which tone and shade can be used on most items in the garden, including the structural elements, the decoration, the furniture, the accessories, and the foliage and flowers of the plants. The whole scheme should be borne in mind when you are planning, so that a single element does not spoil the appearance of the whole garden by looking awkard or out of place.

Using shade and tone

Colour can be a wonderful tool for linking the interior and exterior spaces. An important consideration when using colour, however, is the effect of sunlight or naturally brighter light in washing out tones. A pale tone inside would be far less obvious in the garden. It may be necessary if you want to match tones inside and out, to slightly darken or strengthen the exterior shade.

White should be used carefully in the garden, particularly on a roof where it can glare without mercy. It would be far better to use a pale cream, which will appear softer and be more comfortable on the eye. This rule also applies when using colour on furniture and other features.

Visual effects with colour

Hot colours such as red or yellow draw the eye and tend to foreshorten space. Cool pastels do just the opposite. An orange parasol or tablecloth at the end of a roof or terrace will immediately draw your attention, causing the eye to ignore everything in between. A pastel scheme, however, will diffuse the light, be less obtrusive and increase the apparent space. Use bright hues with care, preferably close to the house or as part of a main viewpoint or point of emphasis.

Of course, these rules also apply to wherever you are placing plants in any garden, whether at ground level or on a roof or balcony. A multi-coloured bed of bulbs or bedding plants might look better near a plain wall than it would close to a brightly coloured wall.

Above left Colour can bring both drama and harmony to virtually any design situation. A patterned floor, shown here with both strong diagonals and apparent verticals, works in much the same way as do carpets inside the house.

Left A simple floor is undemonstrative and easy on the eye, allowing the visual action to take place elsewhere. This is a wonderfully quiet space, brought to life by those people using it.

Right Colour can be cool, hot, fun or simply asking for attention. Although this composition certainly belongs to the asking for attention group, it works well with the carefully chosen combination of planting in pots.

Structure

Planning...

The layout of your garden will depend to a large extent upon the underlying structure. Rather than regarding this as a constraint, you should look on it as a starting point and an opportunity to exercise your ingenuity to the full.

...and building

Once the layout is finalized the creative work itself can start. Whether you have designed your own garden, or it is being built for you by someone else, this is a fascinating process. The structure is the skeleton on which you will hang the plants at the next stage.

Left Where space is limited it is a real bonus if one major feature can double as another. A seat and a raised bed are not only the perfect combination, but also create an interesting visual feature.

Surveys

There are two types of survey: structural and dimensional. The primary function of a structural survey is to find out the load-bearing capacity of the underlying structures. A structural survey by an architect or structural engineer will show how your boundaries – walls, fences or railings – are fixed, what condition they are in and what you must do to meet local building, planning and safety codes. The survey may include a structural drawing detailing the areas involved and specifying the weight tolerances of each area. Avoid anyone who refuses to give you a detailed written report or employs such methods as jumping up and down on a roof to test its strength.

Elements of the survey

Safety is the first consideration when planning any kind of space above ground level. The purpose of the structural survey is to ensure that everything is as safe as possible.

Cost

Cost is always a major factor when taking on any project and a roof garden, area for area, will be more expensive than a garden at ground level. Budgets should therefore be set accordingly and, if necessary, phased over a period of time. Making an accurate estimate is so important that you may wish to seek professional advice.

Barriers

As well as checking the condition of any existing fences, walls and railings, it is imperative to determine how any new barriers can be built or fixed, taking into account the extra weight or leverage that will be imposed on them by the wind.

Load-bearing areas

These are generally around the edge and above internal supporting walls which can transfer the weight down to the ground. These are the areas where you will have to position such heavier items as planters, seating, groups of pots, dividers and water features: placing these on weaker areas of the roof may result in disaster.

The result of the survey

If the proposed surface looks unlikely to accommodate your plans, it may not mean that all is lost

Above left Water is a delightful element in any garden. Where there are weight constraints, small features, such as this spout tucked behind shiny Kiwi leaves, are an ideal compromise.

Left As a general rule the strongest parts of a roof are around the perimeter, where the main load-bearing structure connects with the walls. This is usually where the heavier elements can be positioned.

Right At ground level a sloping site can be terraced into a series of level platforms, each one of which can be paved or planted in a different way. Here, the verticality is emphasized even further by the overheads on the top terrace.

Above Structural elements such as walls, overhead canopies or pergolas can provide the perfect vehicle for a range of climbers, softening the outline of each plant.

or that it will be impossible to create a living space there. Where direct loadings onto the roof are inappropriate it may be viable to construct a surface that is completely or partly suspended on a separate floor, with the weight carried onto surrounding walls or other sufficiently strong areas.

If the survey is positive then you can start to think about just how you will plan your garden, although make sure that you follow advice on the load-bearing potential of specific areas.

The dimensional survey

A scale drawing prepared by a professional will inevitably save you a good deal of time, but doing a dimensional survey for yourself is not only a relatively straightforward and logical job but also a vital stage in the preparation of a design drawn to scale. You will need to measure the area and check a number of other factors that will determine the way in which you use the space.

Again, don't just draw a sketch on the back of an envelope and ignore anyone who suggests that such an approach is acceptable. If you intend to employ a professional, always ask to see examples or photographs of their work before you commission anything. If a professional comes with a recommendation, so much the better.

Tools

To undertake a dimensional survey, you will need certain tools. These include a 30m (100ft) tape measure, a shorter steel tape for measuring short runs or awkward details, a brick or other heavy object to anchor the tape in place as you unreel it, a clip-board and paper, a sharp pencil and a magnetic compass. If the project area is unsafe, perhaps without railings or walls, you may prefer to enlist the services of a professional surveyor.

What to include on the rough drawing

Start by sketching the area of the roof or balcony, noting the positions of doors, windows and projecting walls as well as any drains or drainage channels. Check whether there are any steps or changes in level and mark these as well as any overhanging structures that could affect headroom or planted areas below.

Access is a prime concern and while it may be fun occasionally to scale a ladder to the roof above, this cannot serve as a permanent solution. Remember too that materials for building works may have to come up through the house, so that a well-constructed stairway will make sense in terms of practicality and safety. When constructing the garden, it may be possible to haul materials up to the roof, but you not only need the correct tackle but it will have to be properly secured. A realistic appraisal of all access points to the area and the materials that it will be feasible to carry up through access points could make a big difference to the eventual cost of the project.

Nearly all roofs, even flat roofs, are built to a slope or 'fall' which is designed to carry rain water away, usually into drains or gullies. Check the direction of the fall, as it will almost certainly determine where the excess water from raised

beds will be directed and may even determine where the beds are sited. Nothing which might impede the flow of water must be placed over or in gullies. If water is allowed to stand on a roof it will eventually find its way through.

Services

There may well be existing taps or power points, which should be marked onto the plan since they represent important services that can be extended to other areas of the roof. Power and water are essential. They may be present on the roof before you start work but, if not, they must be installed. Power is needed for lighting and for features such as pool pumps, barbecues, automatic awnings or computerized irrigation systems. Water is the life-line for planting, and as conditions can be harsh on a roof garden you will need easy access to it.

Both electricity and water should be installed by experts, although their positioning should be your decision. At this stage in the project your priority is ensuring that power is available.

Once you have completed the outline drawing you can start to take the measurements. This will involve setting out one or more base lines that

Above Large pots and containers can be very heavy, especially when full of wet soil. Here they are grouped around the edge of the roof, where they also help visually to soften the surrounding walls.

Below It is advisable that services, such as water and electricity, should be professionally installed. They should also be successfully concealed wherever they are installed on any roof, balcony or terrace. As an integral part of any scheme, lighting needs to be a subtle as well as valuable component.

MEASURING THE AREA

Whether undertaken by yourself or a professional, an accurate survey is vital to the planning of any space.

MAKING AN ACCURATE PLAN

Triangulation is a simple exercise in geometry, used by surveyors in order to get an accurate fix on corners.

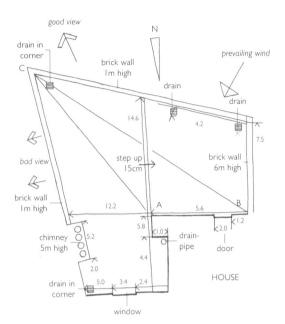

Above The survey plan should be drawn up in the garden to note down all the measurements taken and any other factors such as overhangs and wind direction that are likely to affect the finished scheme. Accuracy is all-important, as any discrepancies at this stage could lead to expensive mistakes later on.

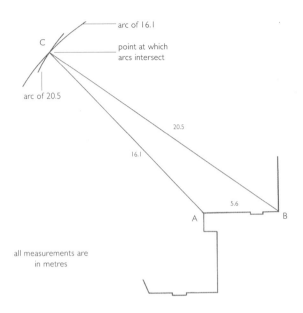

Above To position the third corner of a triangle, plot the two other corners and then, using a compass, draw an arc the correct length from each, i.e., 16.1m from A and 20.5m from B (*see detail above and plan above left*). Where the two arcs intersect is the position of C. Further corners can then be positioned using the same technique.

run along the faces of the building. Anchor the tape at one end of the run, reel it out in a straight line along the face of the building and continue to the end of the wall, across any open space, and fix at the opposite boundary. This is the first base line. Leave the tape on the ground and then take 'running' measurements along the line of the tape, taking in every salient point or feature – for instance, corners, pipes, steps, doors or drainage gullies – along the way. The tape can then be reeled in and re-positioned at right-angles to the position of the first base line, or elsewhere to set up a second base line running in another direction until the whole area is covered.

Roof gardens are quite often awkward in shape, with all kinds of nooks and crannies, which should all be carefully measured. The roof may also be out of square, as shown (*above left*). To fix the corners accurately you need to carry out the simple surveying technique known as triangula-

tion (*above right*). Any steps or sharp changes of level can also be noted and these drops are perfectly easily measured with the steel tape.

Once the basic measurements have been completed you can start to detail the rest of the area. Your surveyor may have indicated what the floor is made of, but if not, you should note it. It could be lightweight or conventional tiles of some kind, paving slabs, roofing felt, chippings, decking or artificial turf. Look at surrounding walls, screens or fences in a similar way, and as well as measuring exactly where the runs are and their height, note the materials they are constructed from.

Don't just survey within the confines of the area but look beyond where there may be good, or quite possibly unattractive, views. Indicate on your survey the exact direction of any such views. These may include a superb distant vista over the city, a neighbouring wall with windows which might compromise your privacy, or a wonderful roofscape that forms a geometric jumble of slates, tiles and chimneys. Chimneys might be an attractive addition to your landscape, but television aerials or satellite dishes will need to be shown on the survey so that they can be screened.

Overhanging roof structures can present particular problems in aerial gardens, as they can either create a 'rain shadow', which starves the area below it of moisture, or have the opposite effect, allowing water to pour onto a bed and create impossible growing conditions.

Another factor to take into consideration is the wind, which is usually stronger at roof height than at ground level. Wherever you live there is usually a prevailing wind that blows from a particular direction for most of the year. In a city, this direction may be modified by surrounding

Above Water is an infinitely variable medium, from grand pools at ground level to lightweight bowls and fountains on a roof. Here water spills from one level to another on a stone-clad terrace.

Below Barbecues and cooking areas should be carefully positioned in relation to the dining area and relevant services. Remember that any open fire is potentially dangerous on a roof.

roofs and buildings, but it will still come from a given point. However, those same buildings may funnel a wind, accelerating it, or creating buffeting as the air finds its way between various structures. Once you have established the direction of the prevailing wind, mark it on your survey, as this will determine how you site screens and organize the living spaces.

The final vital piece of information, and the one that will drive the whole scheme, is where the sun falls throughout the day. Make a note of this early in the morning, at midday and in the evening, drawing an arc on your survey so that you can see the sun's position at various times. Remember that the sun is lower in the winter, with longer shadows than on hot summer days. Note where surrounding walls or buildings cast shadows as this will determine the choice of planting and whether or not you sit in sun or shade at different times of the day. This survey should take you several days or more; it is sensible to take your time over the survey as design ideas often take time to formulate and the longer you spend looking at the space and surroundings, the more you will appreciate what they have to offer.

Above Gothic architecture in gardens is undergoing a revival at present. It is perfectly suited to heavy planting that can heighten the visual drama, such as this *Clematis* 'Prince Charles'. Make sure that any greenery can be moved away from walls for maintenance.

Making a scale drawing

Once you have completed the survey you are ready to transfer the information to a scale drawing. This will be the basis of your final design and allow you to plan the features, planting and furnishings in accordance with the limitations of the underlying structure. The plan will also be the basis of a total cost estimate.

As with the survey, the preparation of a scale drawing is a straightforward business, but one that confuses many people. Drawing something to scale is simply reducing in proportion all the dimensions of the object, in this case a garden, to a size that can be shown on a piece of paper. At its simplest, if you take a dinner plate that is 300mm (12in) across and draw it on a sheet of paper so that it appears to be 150mm (6in) across, then you have reduced the plate by a scale of 1:2. If you reduced it four times it would be a scale of 1:4, 20 times, 1:20, and so on.

There comes a point at which any further reduction results in an object on paper that is too small to be legible, so choose a scale that is small enough to fit on a sheet of paper but large enough to work on in some detail.

In the case of gardens this scale is usually 1:100 (10mm = 1m or ⅛in = 1ft), 1:50 (20mm = 1m or ¼in = 1 ft), or if the area is relatively small, 1:20 or 1:25. In other words, if you work at a scale of 1:50 the garden will be fifty times as large as on the drawing, but everything will be in proportion.

The easiest way to transfer the measurements you took on your survey to create a scale drawing is to work on a piece of tracing paper over a grid or sheet of graph paper. The latter may be a metric or an imperial grid, squared off in centimetres or inches. Use a grid appropriate to the method you chose for measuring the garden.

Before you start the drawing, make sure that the finished plan will fit on your piece of paper by checking the overall measurements and converting them to scale. If the garden measures 10m x 10m and you draw to a scale of 1:50, the finished drawing will measure 200mm x 200mm. If the garden measures 40ft x 20ft, then by using a scale of ¼in to 1ft the drawing will be 10in x 5in.

Tape the graph paper down on a board or table and then tape a sheet of tracing paper over it. Starting from near one of the corners, number the grid in metres or inches up and across the sheet. Now take your survey drawing and transfer the measurements you took onto your scale drawing. So, for instance, looking along that first base line running across one side of the roof, the door was 1m in from the boundary, the end wall 4.5m, the step 7m and the far boundary 12m. Now transfer the measurements that ran in the other direction, mark in the positions of the drains, angles of walls, taps and such things as a skylight set in the ceiling of the room below. Now mark the positions of the good and poor views, the direction of the prevailing wind, and of course the north point. Soon you will have a complete drawing, showing the roof area in miniature, but to scale. This will be the valuable basis for any design. Do not draw directly onto this survey

A SCALED SURVEY DRAWING

Smaller and especially awkward areas, such as corners, may need to be looked at in more detail.

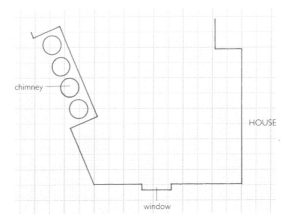

Above Because of their nature, many roof gardens have all sorts of awkward corners caused by such features as chimney stacks, that have to be measured and subsequently drawn up to scale. Such spaces can often form a self-contained area that could be given over to built-in seating, a dining area, raised beds or overhead beams, smothered with climbers.

Above At ground level, load bearing is far less of a problem than on a roof or a balcony. These heavy overheads and columns have been placed effectively in a classical setting to provide a break between the sitting area and the rest of the garden.

drawing but take plenty of photocopies and file the original away for safekeeping.

Like any garden or any room inside the house, the area will be made up of a number of separate elements: essentially the boundaries, floor and ceiling. While the first will be built to provide safety, screening from intrusive views and shelter, the second will provide a durable and decorative surface for all kinds of activities. Ceilings are less often considered, but they are an essential element of any roof area project. Normally the 'ceiling' takes the form of awnings or overheads that provide shelter and shade from the, sometimes intense, heat of the sun. The spreading canopies of trees planted in suitably large containers can also help to define the upper limit of an area.

Balconies

Balconies are usually smaller than roof gardens, and the main structural difference between them is that balconies are usually suspended out from the side of a building. This means that the weight constraints will be even more strict than they are for roof gardens, and that you should therefore avoid grouping heavy items in one place where they might put a disproportionate stress on one part of the supporting structure.

Adding a new balcony

It may even be possible, in certain circumstances, to build a completely new balcony without making major structural alterations to the exterior of your home. This is of course a highly technical job and would have to be undertaken by professionals. Such a structure would almost certainly be constructed from timber so as to remain as light as possible, and might be supported with wires from above or solid joinery from below. If construction is possible, it could give you a whole new living area, completely transforming the way in which you think of your space both inside and outside the home.

Left As a general rule, you should never mix architectural styles. Here the clean lines of this balcony perfectly complement the adjoining building.

Above Wrought iron is a strong material that can be fashioned into complex and delicate patterns. However, these railings are almost incidental, being completely smothered by a glorious riot of planting.

Right These tall, wrought-iron Gothic arched railings are simply designed. Their strong vertical emphasis forms the perfect foil for the delicious tumble of wisteria that droops from the balcony level to the ground level below.

Boundaries

The first considerations on any roof garden, balcony or terrace are the boundaries. It may be that these are already in place and have been passed by your architect or structural engineer as being completely safe. There are always local regulations or codes that must be complied with: if in doubt with any aspect of these, consult a professional. Safety is of course the prime concern, and any boundary must be high enough and strong enough to prevent possible accidents. But shelter and screening are also important. You will already have made a note of any prevailing wind. On a roof, wind speeds can be high, causing plants to be both physically damaged and to dry out quickly. Suitable screening, both on the boundaries and quite possibly within the garden, is therefore important, not just to break the force of the wind but also to provide necessary shade. The position and detailing of these screens is very much a part of the design process, although there are a number of other factors to bear in mind.

Above left For safety reasons, attention to detail is all-important on a roof. Make sure that all fixings are secure and regularly checked for wear and tear. If in any doubt repair or renew them immediately. All pots and ornaments near the edges should be fixed firmly.

Left The design of fences can be an art form in its own right and by varying the width and height of boards you can set up all kinds of fascinating rhythms, as well as echoing the background sky scraper! In addition, this fence neatly screens water and electric ducting.

Function and form

The design of a fence will have a considerable effect on a wind blowing against it. A solid fence or screen will force the wind over the structure and cause turbulence on the lee side, whereas a slatted boundary or screen will filter the wind and provide calmer conditions on the other side. The tops of fences can also be angled, which will affect the wind pattern and potential shelter.

While wind may affect the choice and design of a boundary, so will the need to embrace a fine view. This may mean that you keep the surrounding parapet at a relatively low level, high enough for safety but low enough to keep the view. This boundary could be stone or brick, a low slatted fence, a detailed timber or metal railing, or perhaps even plate glass. The boundary is, of course, solid but can be set slightly above the floor level so that at least air flows over and under the structure, thereby reducing turbulence to some extent.

Above Frosted or etched glass can provide maximum privacy, but allow ample light for both plants and people. The glass-topped table continues the theme, while foliage wraps the garden about, softening the boundaries.

An alternative, where the parapet wall is low and you don't wish to raise it further, is to build a raised planter in front of it. This will form a physical barrier, although safety is still a consideration, particularly if children will use the garden.

If the surface is a deck close to ground level, built-in seating may be ideal. The construction and fixing must be solid and secure, using materials that are as durable and resistant as possible to rot and wind. The fence or screen could be tied back to the main structure of the house, or internal trellising, by overhead beams, struts or wires. This will stiffen and strengthen the structure. A screen or fence forming a right-angle is stronger than a straight run. A fence, screen or trellis is

only as strong as the fixing that attaches it to the walls. Great care needs to be taken in doing this, especially if the parapet walls incorporate a weatherproof membrane or damp proof course carried up from the overall floor surface between the cement render and the stone or brickwork. Drilling, screwing or bolting through this may break the membrane, allowing dampness to work through. Although your surveyor may have noticed this, you should always check it yourself.

Posts might be metal, timber, or piers of stone, brick or concrete. Piers will be the most obtrusive as a screen is usually set between them. Timber and metal posts are less noticeable and may be hidden if the screen is carried across their face. Screens could also be firmly fixed into raised planters or seating, which would of course need to be strong or heavy enough to take the loads.

Materials

There is a wide choice of timber: colour and patterns of grain can vary enormously, so see what is available before making your choice. Certain types of timber are more resistant to rot or insect attack than others. Many tropical hardwoods are harvested from non-renewed resources: this destroys valuable rainforest, so always make sure that any timber you use comes from a properly managed resource. Softer woods vary in durability, but it is sensible to ensure that any timber you buy has been pressure treated with a suitable preservative. Additional durability will be provided by further treatment, with a non-toxic preservative such as a clear sealant, stain or paint. If you are in doubt over the timber to choose, the supplier should be able to give good advice, as should an architect or designer. The design of screens often lacks imagination – for inspiration, look at how they are used in restaurants and other public places. All kinds of patterns and thicknesses of wood are available, from chunky rectangular

Left Safety is always important above ground level, but boundaries and changes in level can be elegantly handled. Here timber trellis and posts are teamed with metal rails.

forms to the delicacy of bamboo. Modern treatments could include wire mesh in bright colours, plastic webbing, bent metal or wrought iron, in either contemporary or traditional patterns.

Construction

Slats, trellis or railings, whether vertical, horizontal or diagonal, will need to be set within or fixed to a secure framework that is in turn fixed to the adjoining building or internal structure. Timber railings, fences and screens have basically the same construction, with posts that are topped and bottomed with cross-pieces or rails laid flat. For fences and screens these are usually the same width as the posts, which should be no more than 1.8m (6ft) apart. In railings, the top rail is often wider than the posts. The spacing of posts will depend on the overall length of the run, as will the size of the posts and rails, all of which will be defined by local building codes. Top and bottom rails can be notched or mortised into the posts.

Infill slats, which form the body of the fence or screen, may be butted together, which might result in turbulence and greater wind pressure, or fixed with gaps between. While the slat-bottoms are usually at the same level, the tops might be slightly varied in height to set up a rhythm. Trellis panels are usually set between posts. Because of the severe conditions on roof gardens, timbers should be fixed with rust-resistant galvanized, aluminium, stainless steel or copper nails, or with brass screws for ultimate strength.

FENCE STYLES

Boundary treatments should be planned and designed to fit in with the style of your garden.

wood and glass panels

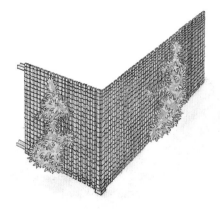

wirebound slats

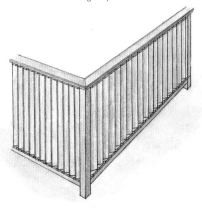

vertical louvres

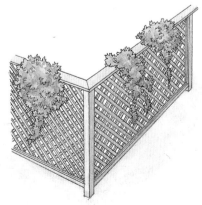

lattice

The floor

The floor is the basis of everything that happens over and under the roof and will have been checked for strength and stability by your architect or structural engineer. Apart from strength, the main purpose of the floor is to stop moisture from reaching the rooms below, and this is achieved with some kind of membrane or damp proof course. The roof's construction may have been carried out in a number of ways: its strength will determine the kind of flooring you use. The strongest roofs can take a conventional garden with all kinds of paving, walling, water features, seating, planting and lawns, although in most domestic situations the layout is much simpler.

Materials

There is a vast range of materials available for flooring and those that you choose should reflect not only the weight-bearing capabilities of your roof but also the amount of use that you may expect each area to receive.

Paving

Conventional paving is feasible if the roof is strong enough, and variations on this include all kinds of natural stone, which can be thinly sawn to reduce weight – various tiles, mosaics, gravels and chippings, and specialized lightweight tiles.

Paving slabs may either be set with open joints on a layer of free-draining gravel over a suitable roof surface, or set on pads or battens to lift them clear of the roof. Each method will allow drainage between the slabs and the roof to suitable outlets. Setting slabs on a continuous bed of mortar should be avoided, as expansion and contraction due to temperature variations might damage the roof membrane below. Smaller modules that are not affected by freezing temperatures can be bonded directly to the roof surface with various mastic adhesives. The gaps between the modules can either be left open or jointed with a flexible filler. Alternatively, expansion joints, which allow the overall surface to flex slightly, should be used no further than 3m (10ft) apart.

Fluid materials

Gravel and chippings of various colours and sizes can provide a low-cost and attractive floor for areas which are primarily decorative. Should access be needed it might even be possible to set

Above left Most floors should have a no-nonsense practical surface that is easy on the eye and does not dominate the surrounding design. Adjoining materials should be carefully detailed.

Left While optical illusions can be fun, they can often become boring and lose their point after a while, so be careful! These topiaried animals are weird and add to the somewhat offbeat composition.

Right Just occasionally you can break design rules with panache. In this situation, stepping stones would normally be neatly rectangular, but there is real power and drama in these rugged slabs.

Above Usually, the lawn and a gravel path would need to be separated to prevent the stones ruining the lawn mower. However, as this lawn does not need mowing, they can be run together.

Below Decking is a completely adaptable material, being easily shaped and fashioned, relatively light, and quickly laid, for both floors and surrounding features and furnishings.

stepping stones through the area. In a 'working' space used for sitting and dining, such an uneven surface would present problems.

More modern surfacing materials include roll-out plastics, plastic tiles, coloured imitation turf and glass beads, which are wonderful for 'non-walk' areas where the sun can make them sparkle.

Decking

Decking is a popular choice. It can be laid to all kinds of patterns and can even be suspended above the main roof structure if the surrounding walls and parapet construction are strong enough to accept the loads and fixings. In this case access should also be considered and simple steps from a doorway at roof level might be needed to reach the new surface. Such a 'suspended' floor might work best in a small area where the joist spans beneath the surface are not too long.

The visual effects achieved through different patterns (*see Chapter 1*) are important. The need to access the roof's surface through the flooring may

need consideration, so rather than building a continuous deck, it may be worth thinking about a deck that is laid in panels or modules. These can be lifted easily, should you ever need to maintain the waterproof membrane or reach drains and services below.

Such modules could be made in sizes from 450mm x 450mm (18in x 18in) to 600mm x 1.8m (2ft x 6ft), but the general rule is that, the larger the module, the more evenly any load is distributed across the roof. From your scale drawing you will be able to plan accurately the size and number of panels needed. If they are all of the same size the pattern will be a regular one, but by mixing sizes, or turning panels at right-angles to one another, you can set up all kinds of interesting patterns and rhythms.

The most straightforward modules use 50mm x 100mm (2in x 4in) boards and these should be of a structural grade and pressure treated. The cleats, to which the boards are nailed or screwed, should have the same dimensions.

If the roof has only a slight slope, the panels may be placed directly onto the surface, provided that drainage is maintained. If the fall is steeper, you can level the panels by using long lengths of 150mm x 50mm (6in x 2in) timber 'sleepers' beneath the cleats. These sleepers can be brought to level by using wedges or 'shims' fixed to the roof with exterior construction adhesive.

The maintenance of drainage beneath the deck is essential, so any sleepers or supporting structures must allow water to run into the drains provided, usually by running these parallel with the roof fall, but if necessary by leaving suitable gaps within the support network.

Of course an entire deck, rather than simply individual modules, can be laid, once again on a framework that will lift it clear of the roof and bring it to the same level. Such a framework of joists or bearers must be spaced closely enough to prevent the deck from sagging or flexing unduly when in use. The joists, which should be pressure treated with preservative, can also be laid upon strips of bituminized roofing felt, which will help to prevent them rotting.

LAYING DECKING

Above The basis of any deck is a strong underlying framework of timber joists that are spaced with regard to the thickness, weight and flexibility of the finished surface, and then positioned across the entire area to be covered.

Above In order to allow drainage beneath a deck, the joists can be lifted slightly proud of the roof surface on blocks or spacers. If the underlying roof slopes slightly, blocks or spacers can also be used to bring the deck level.

Above Boards are fixed last, with non-ferrous nails or brass screws, while removable spacers ensure even gaps. These deck boards are slightly ribbed, to provide extra grip in the wet, and as they are pressure treated they will last for many years.

Heavy elements

The placement of heavy items on a roof garden, balcony or raised terrace is an integral part of the design process, but these elements must be placed where the roof is strong enough to bear their weight. Whatever feature you are considering, all of the loadings should be checked with your architect or structural engineer. Involve professionals in the initial calculations and implementation of the project. Additionally, planters and raised beds, as well as water features, should be designed in such a way that the risk of leakage onto the substructure of the roof is minimized.

Raised beds and planters

Planting brings the roof garden to life but must be treated in quite a different way from planting at ground level: everything must be geared towards keeping the roof watertight and preventing the weight of wet soil from leading to structural problems. On large roofs and commercial projects, planting is often placed directly over the roof, but in such situations the substructure has often been planned specifically to accept it. Although a waterproof layer or membrane can last as long as the building, one leak could mean that the whole of the roof garden has to be removed to locate it. In a private roof garden, plants are often better in raised beds or containers that can be built or placed as units separate from the roof itself.

Layout

The layout will have been determined at the design stage, taking the result of the structural survey into account. As the beds will almost certainly be the heaviest items in the garden, they

Above left Water is a heavy element and needs positioning with great care on a roof or balcony. It makes sense, therefore, to choose a smaller feature that can be an attractive feature in itself.

Left While there are roof gardens that have been built to specifically handle heavy loads, this kind of composition, with substantial planting and water, belongs at ground level in a domestic setting.

Above Brick- or block-built raised beds can also be extremely heavy, although a lightweight soil or compost mix will reduce loadings on the roof. Advice from an architect or structural engineer will be vital before any construction is undertaken.

should, of course, be positioned over the strongest parts of the roof. If in any doubt, go back to your survey, or consult your engineer or architect.

Materials

Materials can echo those used elsewhere and could include brick, stone or concrete, with suspended bases to keep soil and drainage mediums clear of the roof. Timber can also be used in a wide range of designs, as well as plastic, metal and fibreglass boxes or containers. The bed will need

to be waterproofed and to allow drainage onto the floor below and into existing gullies.

Brick or stone can be painted on the inside with a bituminous sealer, which will help prevent water from working out through the wall with possible subsequent staining. These beds can be fitted with a false bottom of pressure-treated plywood, or galvanized metal sheet drilled to allow water to drain freely through. This base will provide protection for the roof surface should you need to empty the bed by using a spade or other tools. Lightweight concrete blocks can be cement-rendered and painted to match the colour scheme, and then painted inside with a bituminized sealer. All such beds should be built with drainage gaps or holes at the base to allow water to drain freely onto the roof. The height of the beds can vary and will depend on the strength of the roof. A good depth of soil or growing medium is between 300mm (1ft) and 450mm (18in), placed over a water-permeable woven plastic membrane that separates it from a drainage layer. This layer could be 150mm (6in) of lightweight expanded clay granules such as 'Leca'. All of this should be positioned over the perforated bottom of the bed which should sit above the roof surface by no less than 50mm (2in) to allow for free drainage. The height of these three layers results in a bed that is a comfortable sitting height.

A growing medium has recently been produced of light, easily handled fibre blocks, that can be fitted into any bed. One of its advantages is that it can be used in layers as thin as 100mm (4in), and still support excellent shrub growth. It is still placed over a drainage layer but is irrigated from below, unlike conventional soil mixes. A water pipe is laid into the bottom of the drainage layer with a float switch and overflow pipe about 40mm (1½in) above. The water is drawn through the fibre into the root system by capillary action. Such a technique could be used in a raised bed,

Left Provided that the roof is structurally sound, you can certainly position relatively heavy features, especially around the perimeter. Overheads and planters have been colour-matched for continuity.

RAISED BEDS

Heavier and larger beds are possible at ground level

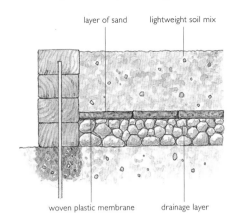

layer of sand · lightweight soil mix · woven plastic membrane · drainage layer

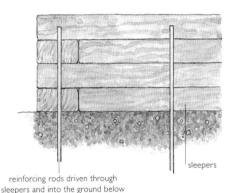

reinforcing rods driven through sleepers and into the ground below · sleepers

Above Railway sleepers (ties) are naturally heavy, so they are best used at ground level. They should be overlapped, like bricks in a wall, and for added strength drilled to accept steel rods that can be driven into the ground.

Above Low-level raised beds can become part of an interesting floor pattern, and their relatively low weight can make them suitable for areas where load bearing is a problem.

Above Until you notice that there is a fountain in the background, you might well mistake this pool for a more conventional raised bed, A contained water feature such as this provides the ideal environment for water-loving plantings, such as umbrella plants and water lilies.

CROSS-SECTION THROUGH A POND

A pump can introduce interest to any water feature.

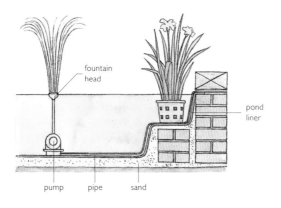

Above Most pumps recirculate water within the pool, cutting down on water use. However, ponds should still be topped up regularly.

with polystyrene blocks making up the height difference, or directly on the protected roof surface.

Timber beds provide the ideal visual link with a surrounding deck. They should at the very least be lined with heavy-duty polythene or butyl rubber, tacked to the inside and perforated at the bottom for drainage, but this is a temporary plan, unless carried out with care. Ideally, they should be fitted with fibreglass inserts, with drilled bases, that can be dropped into position and filled with layers of soil and drainage medium.

Built-in furniture

The last permanent feature, apart from incidental items such as water or barbecues, is any built-in furniture. This can often be a great space saver, being designed as an extension of the basic garden structure of raised beds, screens or boundary treatments. The style and materials should reflect those used elsewhere in the garden.

Water features

Any pool or water feature should be sited in an open position, away from overhanging trees. When first filled, pools will turn green with the action of algae, but will clear again once plants and fish are introduced and a balanced aquatic environment is achieved. Good aquatic or garden centres will sell collections of plants and fish to

Above Small water features are ideal for a roof garden or balcony, providing delightful focal points. Many of these can be bought ready-made and are easy to install.

suit a given size of pool. A submersible pump can be used to give the water movement and to provide aeration for plants and fish, so a power supply should be included on your plans. This will also allow for lighting.

Building a pond

Like raised beds, pools or water features are best kept as a self-contained unit separate from the roof, reducing the risk of leakage or accidental damage. Water features in the garden fit into two broad categories: conventional pools with an area of open water; or smaller features set on a wall or in the form of a 'millstone' type of arrangement.

Conventional pools can be either a preformed fibreglass type, in a wide range of shapes and sizes, or constructed from a tough butyl rubber liner. The former are often more successful on a roof as they are virtually indestructible and can be fitted within a raised area of lightweight concrete blocks, timber or brickwork, similar to the beds discussed on pages 71–74. Drainage holes should be incorporated in the base of the outer skin for any overflow or leakage from a puncture, so that water can run off into the roof drainage system.

Liner pools can also be constructed inside a raised area and should be laid over a false bottom suspended by battens clear of the main roof structure. Black is usually the best colour for both fibre glass pools and liners, as it sets up surface reflections which disguise the depth of the water. Steer clear of sky blue or imitatation pebbled finishes, which can discolour quickly with the effects of algae. A depth of 450mm (18in) is ample, and on a roof this can often be considerably reduced.

Pools should be designed as an integral part of the overall design. Where space is limited, the sides of the pool could serve a dual purpose: if built up to about 450mm (18in) and topped with a broad coping, they can double as an occasional seat, plinth for pots, ornaments or utility surface.

If the roof is strong enough, more exotic compositions can include split-level pools or a simulated rock outcrop. The latter can be constructed by specialists from light, painted fibreglass that is almost impossible to tell from the real thing.

CREATING A POND

A pond on a terrace can be larger than one on a rooftop.

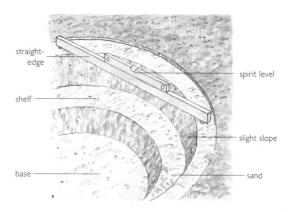

Above The initial excavation will form the marginal shelf and basic outline. The soil should then be 'blinded' with sand and levelled.

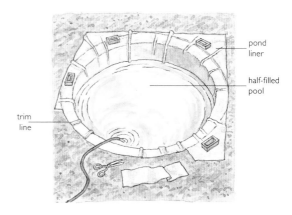

Above Water run into the loosely-fitted liner will mould it to shape. The edges can then be trimmed, allowing enough to hold it in place.

Above The final job is to lay securely the coping and any surrounding paving. The coping should overlap the edge in order to hide it.

Building a terrace

Whether your living space is at high-rise or ground level, it is essential to provide for well-laid, practical and aesthetically pleasing surfaces. The floor will be either bedded directly onto the ground or suspended above it. The materials you choose for flooring, beds, trellises and boundaries, and the design you implement, will have been considered during the conceptual stages (see Chapter 1). As a terrace will usually be larger than a roof garden and will be able to bear greater weights, you will probably have a wider range of materials to choose from.

Boundaries

Since any paved area or terrace needs to be contained, before you lay the floor you should think about the boundaries: walls, fences or raised beds, that will shelter, screen and define the space.

Safety is obviously important and walls of any material – brick, stone or timber such as railway sleepers (ties) or vertically set logs, should be built off sound foundations or 'footings'. These should be twice as wide as the finished structure and taken down to the 'undisturbed' ground. Topsoil should be removed as it is subject to decay, which could cause subsidence. Fences and screens are available in a wide range of styles and the posts can either be set in concrete (*see p.78*) or in spiked metal 'shoes' driven into the ground.

As raised beds at ground level are built differently from those on the roof, they can be set on solid concrete footings. Drainage is essential and pipes or gaps in the stone, brick, blockwork or timber should be incorporated every 900mm (3ft) at the base of the bed, above the surrounding surface. To allow water to percolate freely to the

Above left You can use a greater range of materials at ground level than on a roof, although the rules about simplicity still apply. Here, the grass sits slightly proud of the path so that it can be mowed.

Left Good design is often simple, which does not preclude subtlety. This terrace has all the necessary features: ample paving, a softly planted perimeter and overheads to give light shade.

Above Few of us can aspire to a swimming pool in this kind of setting, with the sight and sound of the sea beyond. Needless to say, sound construction is absolutely vital to retain this area and prevent it sliding into the ocean.

drainage points, a 150mm (6in) layer of broken stone or hard-core should be laid in the bottom. A porous geo-textile membrane between the stone and the upper layer of soil prevents this from washing into and through the drainage layer. A good-quality topsoil should be at least 450mm (18in) deep and can, if necessary, be improved with well-rotted manure or compost.

Retaining walls separate different levels in the garden. While it is possible to build low retaining walls yourself, it is advisable to employ a landscaper, who can work from a structural engineer's

FENCE POSTS

On terraces, one way to set posts is to bed them in concrete.

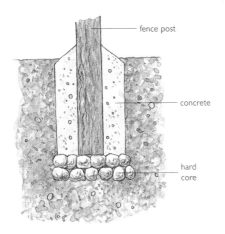

fence post

concrete

hard core

Above Fence posts should be firmly bedded in concrete. Chamfer the concrete just above ground to shed water.

RETAINING WALLS

Retaining walls are ideal for beds at different levels.

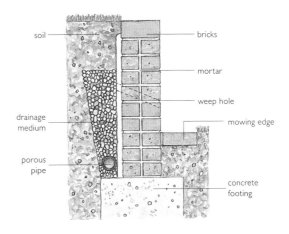

soil

bricks

mortar

weep hole

drainage medium

mowing edge

porous pipe

concrete footing

Above It is essential to relieve pressure behind a retaining wall by incorporating a vertical drainage layer above porous pipework.

drawings, for more ambitious projects. Retaining walls need extra strength because of the pressure of soil and water, and sound foundations are essential. Equally important is the installation of regular drains or 'weep holes' in the wall. Behind the wall a layer of broken stone or coarse gravel allows water to reach the weep holes. Alternatively, a longitudinal perforated drain can be set behind the wall, at the base of the gravel to link into the face drains or to take any excess water

Above Solid timber railings that surround a timber deck or a raised terrace provide visual continuity of materials and are essential for obvious safety reasons.

away in either direction (*see above right*). For added strength, walls can be built from cast concrete with a 'toe' to act as a counterlever at the front face. Such walls can be faced with brick or stone.

Flooring materials

A wider range of materials can be used for a terrace than a roof garden or balcony because of the greater weight tolerances. Materials include cast concrete slabs, gravel, tiles and timber decking.

Paving

Most terraces will be paved, but you need to take a number of factors into consideration. Most houses have a damp proof course (DPC) to prevent ground moisture from percolating up the walls and into your home; if this layer is bridged by paving or other surfaces, such as earth banked up against the wall, damp will work through to the inside. To avoid this, the foundations of any paved area must be laid at least 150mm (6in) below the DPC and paving should be laid to a slope or 'fall' of about 1:100 away from the building. If a terrace is contained by walls or paving at a higher level, drains will need to be incorporated. All paving needs a firm foundation and the first job will be to dig deep enough to accept the finished paving. Allow 100mm (4in) foundation of hard-core or crushed stone, 25mm (1in) of mortar and the thickness of the paving. So if the slabs are 50mm (2in) thick, you will arrive at a depth of 175mm (7in) below the DPC. All of the topsoil should be removed, so you may need to dig further, making up the difference with the foundation layer of compacted hard-core or stone.

As the finished level needs to be laid to a slight fall, drive pegs into the ground to match this on a 1.8m (6ft) grid. Using a long straightedge and spirit level, bring the compacted foundation level with the pegs and 'blind' it with sharp sand or fine gravel to fill in larger gaps before laying paving.

Slabs should be bedded in mortar with four dabs at the corners and one in the middle (*see below*). First bed a slab close to the house, or at the highest point of a paved area, and another slab at the furthest point. Stretch a building line between the two and lay the intervening slabs along this, checking with a straightedge and spirit level as work progresses. A second line should be set up at right-angles to the first, running across the area.

There is a vast range of paving types available. Concrete block paving tends to look utilitarian and is not often chosen for intimate areas. Bricks can be superb provided they are frost-resistant. Special paving bricks can be bedded on a wet or a semi-dry mortar mix (*see p. 80*). In the latter case

Above The character of paving materials can vary enormously, from smooth, polished surfaces that encourage rapid movement, to detailed and textured paving that slow you visually and physically.

the area will need an edge to hold the overall surface firmly in place. This can take the form of bricks set or 'haunched' in mortar, or boards or heavier timbers firmly pegged in place.

Granite setts are cubes of granite once used as street paving. They are available second-hand or new and can make an excellent contrast within a paved area or an edging 'trim' around a terrace or feature, although their uneven finish makes them unsuitable for tables and chairs. They should be firmly bedded together in mortar.

Other small module materials include 'stable paviours', which are usually brick-sized and have an indented pattern; artificial pre-cast concrete

LAYING PAVING SLABS

Laying slabs is straightforward if you follow the rules.

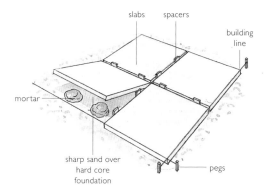

slabs   spacers

building line

mortar

sharp sand over hard core foundation

pegs

Above First a layer of crushed stone or hard core is compacted in. Then five spots of mortar are put at the corners and the slabs aligned with the builder's lines, before being spaced to allow for expansion.

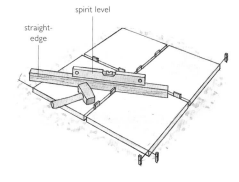

spirit level

straight-edge

Above To ensure that the slabs are at the correct height and are sloped at the correct fall (usually 1:100), use a spirit level on a straightedge and tap the corners down gently with a mallet.

Above Paving at ground level can usually be made of heavier materials than that on a roof and so can include all kinds of natural stone and concrete slabs.

BRICK PATTERNS

Special hard-wearing bricks are now available for paving.

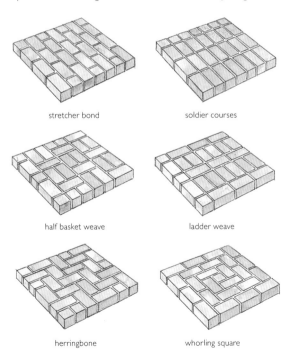

stretcher bond

soldier courses

half basket weave

ladder weave

herringbone

whorling square

Above Bricks can be laid in a variety of patterns, each with a different character. These can create different effects, from the straight lines of soldier courses to the intricate spiral of whorling squares.

'setts' and cobbles. These are egg-shaped stones found on river beds or beaches (it is illegal to remove them, so buy second-hand ones). They can again be ideal as an 'infill' surface and should be packed as closely together as possible.

'Fluid' materials

Materials such as gravel and concrete, which can be cast to virtually any shape, are regarded as 'fluid' and have enormous potential. Concrete can be both elegant and practical. It is a great pity that this material is often under-used and underrated. Its surface can easily be finished in a number of ways (*see p.82, top left*). Some manufacturers specialize in stamping patterns onto the surface of the concrete to imitate bricks, cobbles or other material. While this is often cheaper than laying the real thing, it rarely looks convincing.

Since concrete expands and contracts with changes in temperature, it should be cast as panels with 'expansion joints'. Such panels should be no greater than 3.6m (12ft) square and can become an integral part of the overall terrace design. The expansion joints can be strips of wood, brick, setts or paving slabs. Each panel of concrete must be able to flex independently.

Gravel, provided that it is laid over a well-consolidated base and bedded into a clay binder that is known as 'hoggin', can form an elegant surface, particularly in a traditional setting or small courtyard (*see p. 82, top right*). Gravels come in a range of colours and grades and the paler shades can be used to brighten a gloomy area.

Timber

Timber can be used for a further range of surfaces. Railway sleepers (ties) can form superb paved areas, either alone or contrasted with brick, paving of various kinds or gravels. They are solid and durable and would obviously link into a composition where they were used for raised beds or

Right The soft texture of timber decking always associates well with planting and the staggered pattern of the decking shown here leads you gently across the water to the sitting area.

CONCRETE FINISHES

Even materials usually thought of as plain can be decorative.

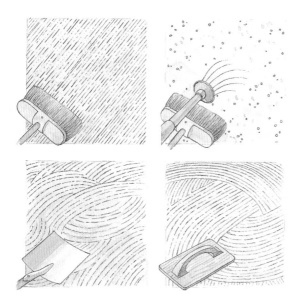

Above Concrete is, in fact, a wonderfully adaptable material and can be given all kinds of surface patterns by brushing or being exposed to show the small stones or aggregate in the mix. Even such articles as spades or a builder's float can create interesting textures.

Above Brick, provided it is hard and 'well fired,' is one of the most versatile and long-lasting pavings. The austerity of this flight of steps is softened by the regular placing of pots.

THE STRUCTURE OF A GRAVEL PATH

The texture and colour of gravel make it an ideal surface.

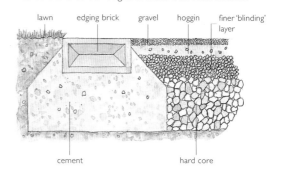

lawn   edging brick   gravel   hoggin   finer 'blinding' layer

cement   hard core

Above Gravel should always be laid on a clay binder, over firmly crushed hard-core, and usually edged to prevent it becoming loose.

steps. Select clean examples that are as free as possible from dirt or oil that can sweat out in hot weather and possibly be carried into the house.

Wood blocks that can be bedded on end in sand are sometimes available. These too are durable and can provide an interesting surface texture. Log slices, sections of tree trunks, approximately 150mm (6in) thick, can also be laid as paving and are usually bedded in sand over crushed stone or hard-core. Such a surface has an informal .character and could blend into a more relaxed part of the garden away from the house.

Steps

Where there is a change of level between paved areas, access will be needed in the form of steps or a ramp. The cue for a choice of materials and style will normally be taken from the terrace, but sound construction is, as always, important.

Steps in a garden should be quite wide, as few things are less attractive or more dangerous than a narrow flight. Proportion is important too, both for the look of the flight and comfort. The ideal measurements are a tread of 450mm (18in) and a riser of 150mm (6in). If the tread is allowed to overhang the riser by about 50mm (2in), it will cast a shadow line and visually lighten the flight.

A long flight of steps may look and feel more relaxing if it has a landing or series of landings. These can often herald a change of direction as well as hosting pots, statuary or other ornaments.

Both planting and water can complement a flight of steps: it may be worth planning the whole feature as an integrated composition.

Methods of construction depend on the amount of traffic expected (*see p. 84*). If this is relatively low, and the ground firm, the bottom riser can be built off a solid concrete foundation with the treads bedded in mortar on excavated platforms running up the slope. A more durable flight can be built with a concrete substructure which is cast into a timber framework or 'shuttering'. Reinforcing rods can be incorporated for added strength. A different finish can then be laid using the concrete foundation as a base.

Steps can be built from different paving materials although timber can also be used. Railway sleepers could work well if used elsewhere in the terrace itself. Logs, firmly pegged, or set vertically into a slope, could provide a less formal look.

Decks

Decks at, or close to, ground level can be even more versatile than those on the roof because there is usually more scope and space available. In visual terms they can form the ideal link between a timber building or interior planked floor and provide an invitation to move outside.

There are also practical advantages, as timber is easily worked to form different angles and fits easily around shapes and into corners where paving might prove awkward.

Before you think about construction, assess your surroundings to see where the deck might best be situated. Microclimate is important, so check where the sun falls. Is a site too hot, or perhaps in the path of a prevailing wind?

As most garden boundaries are only 1.8m (6ft) high, even a low deck could raise you into view of neighbours or the street. You may wish to break the sight lines with screens, either as part of the deck or further away where higher planting could come into its own. Seating, screens and planting around or within the deck will provide a feeling of shelter and intimacy, making the space feel more comfortable. Overheads can be useful, giving privacy, supporting climbers, casting shade, and

providing a visual link between house and garden. When planning the layout make sure that the area is big enough: a deck should be larger than a corresponding room indoors, for ease of access around the space and because most garden furniture is rather larger than its interior counterpart.

It is a good idea to allocate different areas for different purposes, perhaps differentiated by a

Above Roughly hewn stone has been carefully laid to produce an informal flight of steps that allows room for low, cushion planting in between the individual stones.

STEPS

Sound construction is essential for steps.

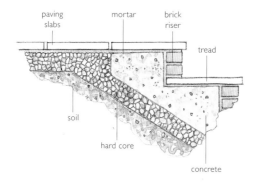

paving slabs — mortar — brick riser

tread

soil

hard core

concrete

Above To achieve a strong, stable flight of steps the treads should be laid off brick risers, over solid concrete foundations, with a good layer of hard core underneath.

change of level, linked by broad steps or screened by raised beds and planting. If they lead out from the rooms inside, so much the better.

Decks can be the simplest and easiest of structures and are easy to build if, for example, they are laid upon bearers over an old paved area or existing unimaginative concrete terrace (*see p. 85*). They can be practical and low in cost, but realize a complete visual transformation of the space.

At the other end of the spectrum, decks can be complicated and sophisticated affairs, soaring

Below This long narrow raised deck is designed primarily to allow access. This function is emphasized by the strong directional nature of the boards and the timber railings.

over a sloping site where platforms could be extended out from the house, linked with steps and incorporate all kinds of features – from built-in seating, barbecues, hot tubs and, of course, planting. Trees and existing vegetation can be worked into the composition, with cutouts in the floor that allow stems or trunks access. A water-side home could provide a magical opportunity to span a deck across a lake or stream, either cantilevered from the building or built on piles from foundations driven into the underlying bed.

Like any structure, work needs to be carried out competently and with care, using professional design and building expertise. Safety and adequate strength are of course essential ingredients and the size and span of a deck will determine just how it is built. As always, timber should be carefully chosen and pressure treated against rot.

Where decks adjoin a building they can be hung from ledger rails bolted to the walls, but in other parts of the garden they may be free standing to form a separate living area. As with any paved area, a deck should always be set to a slight fall away from the building to shed water easily.

Verandas

Verandas are a practical and attractive feature, providing the perfect link between house and garden. In essence they are decks, often right around a building and covered by an extension of the roof. The front is usually left open and the space enclosed by a hand rail. As the height of the deck usually matches that of the floor inside, steps are often needed from the veranda down to the garden, but the change of level is usually slight and the number of steps correspondingly few.

In countries where the sun is high in the sky, it is essential to use any shade to cool both the immediate area and inside the house. If a veranda encircles the home, different parts can be used at different times, depending on the height of the sun. As the area is covered, furniture can be left out, although plants should be watered regularly and the area may be too shady for certain species.

As far as construction is concerned, a veranda is simply a low deck, usually suspended above the

ground on joists and timber piers, those set at the front being used as supports for the hand rails and continuing upwards to carry the roof. Decking patterns can vary, but on the whole should be simple, probably picking up the line and sizing of boards inside the house.

THE ELEMENTS OF A RAISED DECK

A stable, solid structure is essential for a raised deck.

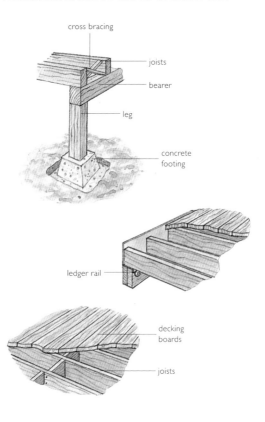

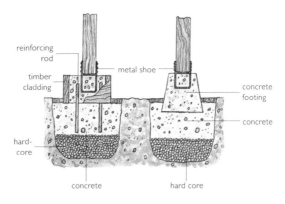

Above A raised deck is an extremely versatile surface, which can create extra levels from a boring flat part of the garden, or turn an unusable sloped area into a valuable extra space. Decks can be placed either near the house or, more informally, away from it.

Overheads and awnings

In addition to wind, the hot sun can cause real problems on a roof – far more so than at ground level, where trees and constructed vertical elements can provide much-needed shade. In addition to providing this escape from the wind, or the sun in the heat of the day, overheads, canopies and awnings can also be useful for breaking the view from neighbouring windows. They can range from the simple to the complicated, from permanent structures with planting trained over them, to retractable awnings or even parasols.

Types of overheads

Overhead structures can be extremely simple, utilizing just a couple of uprights and a few cross members, or far more complicated, for exmple, using slats to echo the patterning of a deck below. They can incorporate screens, which could be set above planters to allow climbers to run over the screens and overheads.

Permanent structures

At their most complex, overheads can be completely roofed in to provide additional shelter, but this can allow debris to accumulate on top. Such debris can be difficult to remove and the result can sound like thunder when it rains.

In structural terms overheads can become part of the support structure for trellises and screens, which can in turn be linked into the boundaries, resulting in the whole fabric of the roof becomes integrated and stronger. Awnings that are reeled out from an adjoining wall can provide both shade and colour, but remember that as wind can be a real problem, fixings will need to be secure to resist especially strong gusts. Awnings should also be fully retractable so that they can be safely stowed away when the garden is not in use.

Movable overheads

At a simpler level any garden centre should stock a range of parasols and sunshades. These are usually sold with their own base and so require only a minimal amount of fixing, with the advantage that they can be moved if necessary.

Above left Overheads need not be complex to look good. The very simplest structures are often the most effective, with slats casting dappled shade below.

Left Many awnings can be automated so that they can be easily reeled in and out. A flexible canvas covering will be ideal for this situation as it will be unlikely to crack along the fold lines.

Right In the final analysis a straightforward manually operated awning may well be the easiest to use, but you should remember that this kind of feature is likely to be vulnerable to gusts of wind when situated on a roof.

Plants

Planning...

Plants are an integral part of your garden's design. They define the visual impact of each part of the garden: their colour, shape, size and texture can be used to bring an area to your attention or to make it fade into the background.

...and choosing

Which plant species you choose will, of course, depend on the style and size of your garden, as well as the climate. The plants form the clothing for the structural skeleton of the garden and your choice should be just as personal to you as your own dress sense.

Left Plants bring any garden to life. Whether the garden is large or small, on a roof or at ground level, plants will enhance the space with their colour, texture and fragrance.

Arranging the plants

Planting in small spaces, including roof gardens, balconies and terraces, is particularly important; too much and the whole area can be swamped, too little and the result can be meagre, emphasizing the harshness of the surroundings. Roof gardens and terraces each have their own particular problems which are largely to do with the severe weather conditions they may experience. However sheltered the space may be, wind will almost certainly prove troublesome at some point. This, combined with a hot sun, can make conditions difficult to deal with.

Plants to suit the conditions

This tends to suggest that certain species are more successful than others, although with care, and a lot of hard work, you can grow nearly anything on a roof or in a container. As a general rule, many Mediterranean plants do particularly well in these circumstances, being largely resistant to drought and adapted to thrive in hot, sunny conditions. Such plants often have felt-like or tough leaves that slow down their rate of transpiration.

Frost is far less likely to attack plants at higher levels. Although conditions may be tough, they are far from impossible, and you may even be able to grow species that would not survive in colder conditions elsewhere. One of the great joys of gardening lies in achieving something that others find difficult, so think and choose positively.

Nurseries and plant catalogues are very good sources of information on plants suitable for particular climates. Those plants which tolerate a specific range of conditions will naturally do better than those whose natural habitat is different from that of a proposed site. Bearing this in mind, a well-planted aerial garden is a joy, providing a rooftop oasis which thrives in spite of all the odds.

Successful planting

There is an enormous advantage in being able to choose your own ideal soil mix and in tailoring it to meet the particular needs of the plants you choose. You will, for example, be able to influence the acidity or alkalinity of the soil and so may be able to grow a wider range of plants than if you were in a garden at ground level.

Above left Formal floral settings work equally well inside or outside the home, acting as focal points that both draw the eye and link with the immediate surroundings.

Left Informal planting brings softness to the garden. It relies for its effect on the relationship of leaf texture, shape and form, as well as the overall outline of any given species.

Right Vertical planting will allow terraces to be gently moulded together without losing their architectural outline. The orange of the fruit brings a strong splash of colour to the white wall.

One of the secrets of successful planting is to make sure that beds and containers are as large and as deep as possible. The bigger their size, the more they can retain moisture and provide ample root room for the plants. A larger container also affords protection against extreme cold where the temperature drops below freezing. As well as having large enough containers, successful planting also requires you to spend time and trouble over both the selection and care of the plants.

Plants for all year round

Many people forget about the potential of a garden in winter, but since it can be several degrees warmer on a roof than at ground level, you can usually enjoy the space for a lengthy season. If, however, your garden is only used at certain times of the year, you will want a scheme that comes into its own at a given time, or at least does not look at its best when you are away.

Before we look at plant groupings it would be useful to review some of the principles of planting design that allow material to be put together attractively. Planting design styles can vary enormously. Some revel in the individual beauty of a

Above In this long, narrow area of roof garden, the careful positioning of plants of different heights in large planters interrupts the line of sight, slowing down one's glance along the length of the garden. As a result the garden seems larger than it really is.

plant, others look at the broader appeal of form, shape and texture. Both approaches are valid, but concentrating on the beauty of specific plants will almost certainly use a greater number of species within the garden.

However, I personally prefer to concentrate on form, shape and texture. For me the flower is a seasonal bonus rather than the prime object of a species: as blooms can last only a short time, the rest of the plant has to provide interest for the remainder of the year. Whether you favour one style or the other, bear in mind that the planting of a garden, like the design, should reflect your personality and serve those who use the space.

Making a selection

You need only look at the range of plants at any garden centre or nursery, or in a catalogue, to see how potentially complicated plant selection can be. This can often be compounded by seemingly complicated professional advice. In fact, if the job is tackled in a logical sequence, it is straightforward and immensely rewarding.

The first difficulty is the distinction between classifying the plants and understanding the roles the plants can fulfil in the garden. To clarify this I have summarized below the types of plants available and just what they can do for you.

Trees

The largest plants are trees, and while you don't want something that dominates the area the smaller species can be extremely valuable. They can provide both vertical emphasis and shelter from a prevailing wind, as well as shade. Trees can be grown for their foliage, which can change dramatically from spring to autumn, as well as blossom, fruit, berries or nuts. Small-foliage varieties are often more appropriate in roof gardens as their canopies cast lighter shade and the leaves are less likely to be buffeted by strong winds. Most suitable species of tree are deciduous and therefore lose their leaves during the winter.

Trees occupy the highest storey of planting. They will need to be secured to prevent them from being worked loose by the wind. Shapes vary from fastigiate, or upright, to weeping, flat-topped, contorted or rounded, all of which have a different character and visual emphasis.

Above In this raised wooden bed, the designer has used the colour, texture, height, leaf size, shape and habit of the plants to create an area that always catches the eye. By concentrating on the whole plant, rather than just the flowers, the gardener has ensured that the bed will remain of interest for a much longer period.

RAISED BEDS AND PLANTERS

Raised beds perform a number of functions. As well as providing height so that smaller plants are not always at or below knee level, they allow the gardener to control the acidity of the soil and so grow plants that would otherwise not thrive. Planters for roof gardens are built differently to those for terraces in order to keep the weight down.

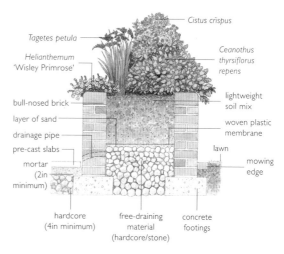

Above This raised brick planter is designed for use at ground level, with a layer of hardcore allowing it to drain into the soil. Root run and water will still be limited: species that enjoy hot, dry conditions will be ideal, as will a combination of medium height and lower-growing, sprawling plants, to soften the walls.

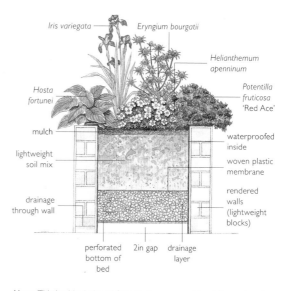

Above This bed is designed for use above ground level. Its rendered walls are made of lightweight blocks and water drains out through the wall. Irrigation is the key to rooftop planting. If carried out properly on a regular basis you can use a wide range of plants, including such water lovers as broad-leafed hostas.

Above Flowers should be a bonus, bringing colour at a particular time of the year. They should always be reinforced with a background of interesting foliage.

Above On a roof garden or balcony, where space is often quite limited, the planting will not only have to bring colour and interest and to clothe screens and walls, but should take up as little space as possible at the same time.

Shrubs

Shrubs have an enormous range of sizes, shapes and characteristics. They can be either evergreen or deciduous, and can be grown for their flowers, fragrance or foliage; they can also form a natural framework into which smaller and more colourful material can be woven. Many shrubs flower prolifically at different times of the year, including winter. While the foliage can provide enormous interest, particularly when contrasted with other species, many deciduous shrubs have an attractive branch structure that comes into its own during the winter, especially if it is set against a suitable background. Many shrubs can be successfully grown in pots and containers, which is a valuable bonus on a roof garden, balcony or terrace.

Hardy perennials

Shrubs have hard, woody stems but hardy perennials (or herbaceous plants) have far softer stems. The majority of hardy perennials die down in winter to reappear the following spring. These are the plants of the classic English herbaceous border and the term embraces a huge range, from stately spires smothered in mid-summer bloom to low ground cover. Although many are grown for their flowers, which can appear in winter as well as summer, many also have handsome foliage.

If a garden were laid out using only hardy perennials, there would be little winter interest, but adding shrubs can make an ideal combination. Hardy perennials can be used in a mixed bed or border to visually lighten the composition, while the shrubs' branch structure lends valuable support. Hardy perennials can also be planted in containers if they are fed and watered regularly.

Annuals

The term annual or, more correctly, half-hardy annual, is applied to plants propagated by seed

Right Box and other hedging plants can act as a wonderfully sculptural material that can take the place of hard landscape materials in an altogether softer context. This display will look equally good in summer or winter.

early in the year that flower during the same summer. Annuals are usually killed by frost at the onset of winter; they often originate in frost-free climates where they last from year to year. The pelargonium of South Africa is one such plant, and can be over-wintered in more severe climates if lifted and kept in a frost-free area.

Annuals are typically grown for their flowers, which can be spectacular and will last all summer if the spent blooms are removed before setting seed. They complement other planting, bringing instant colour and vibrancy, or can be used as 'fillers' in a young border where shrubs and herbaceous material have not knitted together. Their other use is in pots, containers, boxes and hanging baskets, which makes them an invaluable choice in a small area such as a balcony.

Bulbs

Bulbs can be treated either like hardy perennials, which die down and reappear, or annuals, which are removed once they have finished flowering. In the first approach – naturalizing – the bulbs are left in the ground from year to year, in a border where they can be mixed in with other planting to create a vibrant spring display. They are particularly valuable here as few other plants flower this early and many have not yet gained their summer foliage. When the bulbs finish flowering they are allowed to die down naturally before the foliage is removed. The alternative use is to plant them in pots and containers in autumn so that they flower the following spring. Once they have finished flowering they are allowed to die down before being lifted and stored. The pots can then be replanted with annuals for the summer. Different bulbs flower at different times of the year, most in spring but some in autumn. As a group, bulbs are enormously varied, ranging from tiny species only a few inches high to stately daffodils.

Climbers

This group of plants is especially useful in those areas partially or fully enclosed by walls, fences or screens. Most climbers are shrubby: they retain their branch structure in winter and they can be evergreen or deciduous. Although there is a climber for every situation, sunny or shady, they vary in their resistance to frost. Some are grown for their beautiful, often fragrant, flowers and some for their foliage, which varies enormously.

Left The marriage of hard and soft landscape can be both strong and subtle. Low planting has been used between these slabs to produce an interesting chequer-board effect.

There are two main types of climber – those that attach themselves and those that need to be supported. The support can be some kind of trellis fixed to the surface, which can also become an additional decorative element. Alternatively, climbers can be tied into horizontal wires, spaced every 450mm (18in) up a wall or stretched between fence posts.

Fruit, vegetables and herbs

Fruit, vegetables and herbs can be grown successfully in small areas, either in raised beds or pots, or in 'grow bags', which contain a well-balanced compost to ensure optimum growth. Vegetables are valuable as much for their decorativeness as for their culinary potential. Herbs in particular have long been grown for the quality of their flowers and foliage as well as their wonderful fragrance. Both fruit and vegetables can look handsome, especially when mixed with other planting.

Many people dismiss the idea of growing fruit trees in such a limited space as a roof garden, balcony or terrace as impractical, but they can

Above Raised beds and boxes can provide both definition and softness around a small garden, particularly if they spill over to disguise the containers below.

Above With tender loving care, reasonable room and regular feeding, even a roof can be lush and green, screening both surrounding walls and uncompromising views.

work very well in small spaces if miniature varieties are grown on a 'dwarfing' rootstock. Such trees can be grown as miniature bushes, trained as cordons, espaliers or fans or, a more recent development, in a pyramidal shape with a single main stem. If the branches are trained they will take up very little space and can be appropriate for even the smallest balcony. Apples and pears are particularly well suited to this treatment. The single-stem types, of which the 'Ballerina' varieties are a good example, are ideal for growing in a restricted area. As with any vigorous plant, the larger the pot the better. Regular feeding and irrigation is important during the growing season, as is some protection from frost during winter and early spring.

Few apple species are fully self-fertile and so for successful fertilization you will need at least two compatible varieties. Many varieties are partially self-fertile but (as is also the case with pears) a better crop will be formed if pollination is from another tree.

This brief guide classifies broadly the kinds of plants you are likely to use. There are other, more specialist, areas which you may be familiar with or will learn about as your interest develops.

Left A Mediterranean climate naturally brings enough warmth for citrus fruit to grow freely. Such trees grow well in containers, with regular attention, although being confined in containers will often limit their development.

Above Many vegetables have striking form and foliage and should be used in beds, borders and containers more often. Ornamental cabbages are particularly handsome in winter.

TRAINING FRUIT TREES

If space is limited, fruit trees can be trained on wires in a variety of shapes, including cordons, espaliers and fans.

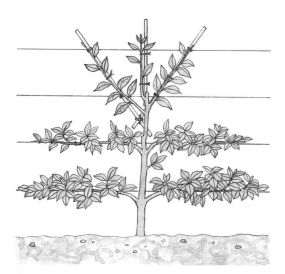

Above Sticks can be used to support angled branches.

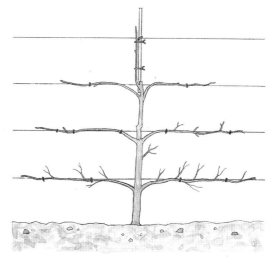

Above Side shoots should be pruned back to maintain the shape.

Pots and containers

Pots and containers play an especially important role in the smaller areas of a roof, balcony or terrace. Where it is difficult to build raised beds, pots can be packed together tightly so that almost the whole area is filled. They need not be at floor or ground level: boxes and baskets can be hung from walls, perched on ledges or placed on sills – always bearing in mind that they must be securely fixed to prevent accidents below. Window boxes can be wired back to the frame on either side or screwed to the sill. Parapet walls, if they are wide enough, sometimes offer the chance to construct integral boxes or troughs on top. Alternatively, long plant boxes can be built into the base of screens so that climbers can scramble up the surface. The plants can complement or enhance the container: an erect plant in a tall urn can act as a strong focal point; or colours could be used to make bold contrasts as, for example, when massed white flowers are set in a black pot.

Above left Pots and containers are the workhorses of roof gardens and balconies. Because of their mobility, they can be positioned to set up all kinds of fascinating patterns and rhythms.

Left Pots can often be grouped in generic types, in this case clay and terracotta. The contrast of different heights, textures and colours brings interest, as does the mix of exotic species, the aloe casting dramatic shadow against the wall.

Selecting containers

Any container, of whatever size, must have ample drainage. Pots bought from garden centres should have drainage holes, but always check. If necessary you will have to puncture the base of the container. Similarly, the bottoms of boxes should be drilled to allow water to drain away.

An enormous range of containers is available: your choice should be in sympathy with the overall style of the garden. The cost of the containers will be similarly variable, ranging from that of an expensive antique to the simplest bowl bought from the local garden shop or to 'found' items: some of the most effective containers started life as something quite different. Often the pot becomes an incidental feature, with foliage and flower spilling out to conceal all below. You don't have to spend a fortune for an attractive display.

While you can certainly mix styles and materials, do not overdo it, as a random collection of anything can tend to look fussy. Choose compatible materials: timber, terracotta and stone are of a similar type, looking quite at ease in a traditional composition. Modern materials such as fibreglass

Above Pots can either be a simple vehicle for plants or, as here, focal points in their own right. Careful positioning will be essential if the overall composition is not to become too 'busy'.

and plastic in bright primary colours are quite different, perhaps looking better beside polished metal or a contemporary concrete façade.

Positioning containers

Containers and other incidental features are an integral part of the design and must not be chosen and positioned in isolation, So that while there is room for some 'found' items, most containers should reflect the overall garden style.

This applies to positioning as well as materials, and while terracotta pots might look at home in a contemporary or traditional garden, they could be placed more formally in a contemporary setting and asymmetrically in a traditional setting *(see p. 103)*. The same approach could apply to wall-hung containers: a formal approach might see identical boxes on either side of a doorway, while informally they could be grouped to one or both sides, in an irregular but pleasing pattern.

WOODEN PLANTERS

A wooden box will be lighter than a similar-sized concrete bed, but is filled in much the same way, with sufficient drainage material to prevent waterlogging.

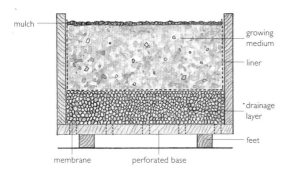

mulch

growing medium

liner

drainage layer

feet

membrane   perforated base

Above A waterproof liner protects the wood from the wet soil.

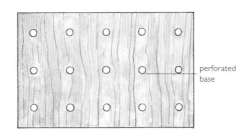

perforated base

Above Plenty of drainage holes should be drilled in the base.

Another guide to grouping pots is to use odd numbers, as three or five looks more comfortable than two, four or six. The classic arrangement of three containers uses one tall and narrow, one broader, medium-sized and a final small pot. This forms a triangular pattern, a familiar shape which is successful in many areas of design.

An advantage of most containers is that they can be moved: rearranging them can change the whole character of a space. Unfortunately, this is something we do indoors, but less often in the garden. Small pots can be moved easily but larger pots may need two people. Alternatively, fit them with castors or put them in a small wheelbarrow.

Size

The bigger the pot, the happier the plant will be, but feeding and watering will also need to be part of the maintenance programme in a way that is

Below The designer of this garden has used colour very cleverly to provide linkage between the building and the garden: white blooms echo the paint of the walls and the shutters reflect the terracotta pots. The muted tones of the paving mediate between the two.

not usually necessary with beds at ground-level. Any container, whether it is a raised bed, a planter or a pot, will tend to limit the eventual size of plants by restriction. Even with regular feeding and irrigation, in such a situation contained plants may fail to reach the size stated in a catalogue or planting encyclopedia. Exposure to especially cold or strong winds may also limit their development.

Large containers can accommodate either a vigorous shrub, a group of smaller plants, or a combination of both. Such an approach would be ideal to provide permanent colour and interest throughout the year, particularly in winter. The combinations of plants will necessarily be far simpler in a container than in a larger raised bed, owing to the limited space available.

ARRANGING POTS

How pots are grouped and positioned has a major effect on the perceived formality or informality of the area.

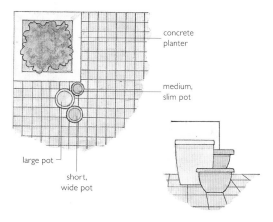

concrete
planter

medium,
slim pot

large pot

short,
wide pot

Above The archetypal informal arrangement of three pots.

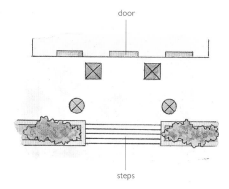

door

steps

Above A symetrical formal composition.

Above Comparable species of plants and similar-looking pots will always look good if they are grouped together. There is great empathy in this cluster of shallow bowls brimming with succulents that leads the eye down through the space.

Above Odd numbers of pots and plants always tend to look more comfortable than even numbers, although if three are all the same size they tend to look more static than an asymmetric trio.

Planting structure

The way in which you structure or arrange your planting is the key to clothing the garden and bringing it to life. Just how you carry this out is dependant on the space available: an expansive roof garden or terrace might have beds of ample size while a balcony may have room only for pots and containers. With a roof garden you can obviously grow a collection of different species, but on a balcony you will almost certainly be dealing with far smaller groups or single specimens. Even so, the pots and plants will need to be arranged in both a sensitive and practical way as the skill of planting design lies in the juxtaposition of shape and texture.

Arranging plants

Before preparing a planting plan check your scale drawing for details about wind, sun and shade, and establish what kind of soil you have or can bring in. A successful planting scheme will take all this into account so that groups and drifts of plants can be positioned so as to complement one another and make the best use of the site.

Drawing up a plan

While some people can plant a garden by eye, for most of us this is a recipe for disaster: it is almost impossible to remember all the details of height, spread, cultural requirements or the relationship of different leaf textures and flower colours.

To make life easier and avoid expensive mistakes, you should prepare a planting plan showing which plant goes where. Such a plan should be drawn to scale and will take your scale drawing (*see p. 56*) as its starting point. Working from a planting plan is essential if you want a sense of

Above left Small-leaved plants can provide infill, cover and colour. Plants such as variegated ivies are quite shade-tolerant, which makes them particularly useful in corners away from the sun.

Left One large plant can serve to soften a hard corner and block a view beyond, allowing lower-growing species either side to provide greater colour and interest.

Above There are some views and positions that should never be obscured, even at the expense of shelter. This bird's-eye view of Central Park in New York is a case in point.

cohesion in your garden. While the occasional impulse buy is undoubtedly fun, avoid making a habit of it, as it almost always leads to a disorganized scheme. Read the label before you buy and note the plant's flowering time, as well as its eventual characteristics and size, so that you can ensure that it will be suitable for the space. Every plant should be drawn on the plan at its final size, which ensures that the scheme will mature into a composition in which each plant has developed without encroaching on its neighbours.

A SUN PLAN

A plan should include details of sunny and shady areas, in both summer and winter.

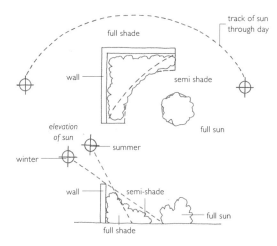

Above The areas of sun and shade dictate which plants go where.

Planting has practical functions, including shelter and screening from winds and poor views. The planting plan will determine the position of these plants as well as the maintenance they will need. A well-planned scheme can knit together and reduce work to a sensible minimum. In general, a scheme should follow the form of planting in a natural environment, with trees at the highest level, shrubs and some hardy perennials as a middle storey and finally a layer of ground cover. Obviously, the smaller the space available the more this approach may need to be modified.

A planting plan builds up logically. Framework plants come first, the trees and larger shrubs, followed by smaller shrubs and herbaceous material and finally the ground covers, annuals and bulbs.

Framework planting

The first and largest elements to position are any trees. In limited areas, choose smaller, less vigorous species, with light foliage to filter wind and block a view without being too dominant. In general these will need the maximum root run, in a raised bed or the largest possible container. While there will be room for only one, or at most a few trees, shrubs are a different matter. These range from larger species that grow to 2m (6ft) or more, down to ground-covers only a few inches high.

Initially you should position the main framework plants to provide shelter and screening and give an overall structure to the space. Many suitable framework plants are evergreen, ensuring winter interest and cover. These are often tough enough to form a protective 'outer envelope'.

A PLANTING STRUCTURE – THE PLAN

A planting plan should be based upon your original survey. It should always folllow a logical structure.

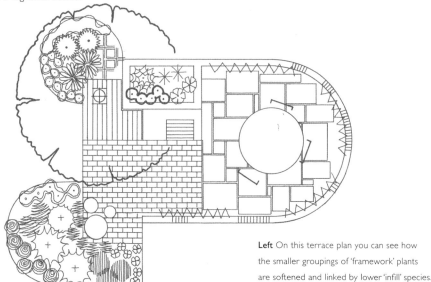

Left On this terrace plan you can see how the smaller groupings of 'framework' plants are softened and linked by lower 'infill' species.

Such planting will not encircle the garden, but will be placed only in key positions for specific purposes. Where you wish to retain a view, and shelter is unnecessary, planting can be lower.

It is important also to consider the outline formed by these larger specimens. It should be visually undemanding: most such plants should form an unobtrusive background on the boundary rather than be a focal point in their own right, which will simply draw attention to where your space ends. Framework plants should be 'softeners', disguising hard edges, breaking the angles of corners and even, if possible, linking with similar plants in an adjoining space or garden, thus making your plot appear a good deal larger.

Leaf size also is relevant here. Large, palmate leaves demand attention and draw a boundary in. Conversely, small, delicate foliage tends to fragment a boundary line and push it away, increasing the apparent space. It therefore makes sense to choose background 'framework' plants that make the plot feel as large as possible.

Above Leaf form is all important in planting design and a fine grass will help to break the line of a boundary by visually pushing it farther away. These grasses add further delight as they rustle in the wind.

Below There is nothing wrong with strong colour, as long as you are bold enough to use it and understand the relationship of the various ranges involved.

Climbers can form part of framework planting as they are often used on the perimeters of an area, helping to conceal the boundary. They are invaluable in clothing screens and dividers, blending them gently into the overall composition: climbers can also be allowed to run up and around the adjoining building; a green background is obviously more attractive to look at than brick or concrete.

FRAMEWORK PLANTS

Careful planning is needed to achieve a graduated arrangement of plants.

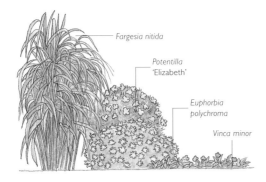

Fargesia nitida

Potentilla 'Elizabeth'

Euphorbia polychroma

Vinca minor

Above Many planting schemes work well with screening and structural plants towards the rear of a border, more colourful infill material in the middle and ground cover at the front. (*See also the plan on p. 106.*)

Above In a well-balanced garden border, whether at height or at ground level, there is a subtle contrast and grouping of species in layers that will provide interest over a long period, using texture, leaf form and shape as well as colour.

Filling in

Now consider how the intervening spaces can be filled with medium and small shrubs and herbaceous material. In drifts, the number of species can be higher, perhaps with one gently leading the eye through and past a sharp angle, or reinforcing a curve. Alternatively, plants can emphasize a geometric shape or underlying pattern, especially if they are clipped in a regular outline.

While framework shrubs are nearly all tall, infill plants can vary in height and shape and need not be rigidly graded from tall at the back to low at the front. Higher planting, often herbaceous, in the middle of the border, can highlight points of interest and give vertical emphasis. Ground-cover plants can include shrubs, hardy perennials or annuals, and can be used in greater numbers still, sweeping beneath taller material and linking areas containing several species.

Think about contrasts in leaf shape and texture, flowering lines and the difference between evergreen and deciduous material. The overall shape of the plant is important – is it rounded or spiky, feathery, prostrate or fastigiate? There are classic combinations such as a fastigiate or spiky shape behind a rounded outline, or sword-like leaves driving through large, round leaves. Finely divided leaves can look handsome with broad, bold foliage, while a horizontal sweep of ground cover can tie together complex forms above.

You can gain inspiration from many sources, the best of which are real gardens rather than flower shows where plants can be grouped unrealistically. Always carry a notebook and camera and make notes on plant height, spread, soil type, flowering time, etc., to build up a personal portfolio of plants. Botanic gardens are a useful resource for plant associations and accurate nomenclature, but you will often find that domestic plots similar to your own have other practical ideas to offer.

Right Architectural features benefit from the softening influence of plants. Here, in a courtyard, the arching lines of the delicate palms lead the eye up in sympathy with the rising staircase. There is no need for added colour in the plants here.

Colour

While colour is normally thought of in terms of flowers, bloom is usually the most vibrant feature and often one of the main reasons for choosing a particular plant in the first place. But you should not forget the bonus of the additional palette that leaves and berries provide with their changing colours at different times of the year. Colour, unfortunately, tends to be one of the most badly misunderstood and mismanaged elements in the garden, as a result of which one quite often sees gardens containing jumbles of unrelated hues with little or no continuity.

Above left Colour is one of the designer's most vital tools, drawing the eye or allowing a scheme to recede gently into the background. By demanding attention, these vibrant, urgent hues tend to foreshorten the space between themselves and the onlooker.

Left This scheme has been carefully worked in shape and texture, together with subtle colour grading, which is essentially cool with just a dash of hotter shades. It certainly would not benefit from any additional colour.

Above There is never just one, but literally thousands of shades of green, yellow or any other colour. This is why schemes that largely rely on foliage and cooler colours can be intricate as well as delicate.

Colour management

The basis of colour management is understanding the difference between the hot and cool ranges, and what these achieve visually. An understanding of the effects of different colours, shades and tones will help you to use them logically.

Positioning colours

Gertrude Jekyll was a painter before she took up gardening seriously and she brought with her an artist's understanding of colour in the landscape. It was her perception that hot colours – reds, yellows and oranges – are naturally vibrant and draw the eye. Conversely, blue, pink, mauve and pastels are cool and increase a feeling of space. It follows that hot colours at the furthest point of any area demand attention and the eye tends to ignore much of the intervening space. This has a foreshortening effect and the garden, or part of the garden, feels smaller as a result. The way to create the maximum possible feeling of space is then to grade the colours, from hot colour in the foreground or close to the house to the cooler colours in the distance.

Above This is a superb example of planting design at its best, with a glorious grading from white, through the flowering grass to the gorgeous warmth of the *Coleus* in the foreground.

Grey is a moderating agent that can link colour ranges and tone down vibrancy and settle it into cooler surroundings. A stunning red rose, which might be too dominant in a small area, could easily be tempered by the addition of grey foliage. Cream flowers would reinforce the subtlety and the result could be breathtaking. Paradoxically, toning down a striking colour in this way does not negate its effect but makes more of it, the addition of a secondary colour highlighting the first.

To prevent a pastel colour scheme becoming bland, add a measured splash of colour from the other end of the spectrum. You do not need a great deal: the amount is something you have to judge by eye and experience.

White can be used to add 'highlights' within a scheme, often to add sparkle to colours at the heavy end of a range. In this way a sweep of copper, purple or another dark colour can be given a delicious fillip with the purest white.

Tonal ranges

There are thousands of shades of red, yellow or green, each with a slightly different role. When studying landscape, I was taught to appreciate these subtle differences with a complex paint colour chart, trying to match a plant species to each. This was a nightmare exercise but it made me realize the diversity of the plant palette. The point here is that using colour to advantage in the garden is no different from using it well in any other sphere. There is no separate set of rules for outdoor designers: the same instincts which govern our choices at home and at work should be allowed free reign in outdoor spaces.

The effect of sunlight

Every gardener appreciates the effect that light has – not only on colour but on the garden in general. Anyone who has observed a climate different from their own will appreciate the effect that stronger or softer light has on a landscape. The stronger the light, the more it tones down colour. In very strong light, hot colours lose their vibrancy, or at least look less dominant. In tropical and sub-tropical countries there is a higher proportion of brightly coloured blooms, which would stand out in sharp relief in the more softly coloured landscapes of temperate areas. Where plants native to one country are introduced to others there is a possibility that they may clash with their surroundings. The misty backdrop of an English garden is often best suited to the subtleties of pastels, rather than the urgency of hot colours, but a plot in the Mediterranean could look very drab without the drama and vibrancy of its bright native blooms.

Light values are often higher in roof gardens and balconies, so you can use correspondingly stronger and harder colours without their necessarily dominating everything around them.

Above White is one of the most telling hues, with the ability to brighten a dark corner or highlight any part of a border. There is a purity about white that sets it apart from other colours.

Left Spring is the season of hope and regrowth after the winter, with instant and welcome colour being provided by bulbs and other early flowers. Foliage is at its freshest and brightest with the vibrancy of youth.

Above Because pink and blue are in the same colour range, this tumbling pink fuchsia and the dark blue lobelia underplanting combine to make the perfect pair.

Planting and care

All plants need a growing medium, water and nutrition. The first, soil, compost or rockwool, is the material in which plants anchor themselves and which carries the moisture and nutrients to the root systems. The medium you choose depends upon the load-bearing potential of the roof or by the ease with which material can be imported from ground level. Depths of soil will vary depending on the type of planting you choose, and while a large raised bed would need a depth of 450–600mm (18in–2ft), a pot of bulbs may need only half this amount or less. The amount of water and nutrition that your plants need will depend upon their size, as well as the size of their pots and the climatic conditions.

Planting media

Ordinary, good-quality topsoil is used only on the strongest roof gardens or those which have been purpose built to take heavy loads. It should be friable with an open structure and is best obtained from a reputable supplier. In most instances, you should opt for a compost based on peat or coir, both of which are much lighter. Bear in mind that composts straight from the bag are virtually dry, and when wetted down will be a great deal heavier, adding to the loading on the roof. Peat-based composts are slightly acidic and therefore best for plants that enjoy these conditions. There is, however, some controversy about the use of peat, as its extraction destroys environmentally sensitive sites. You can increase the acidity of any growing medium by adding proprietary acidifiers or buying a specially prepared 'ericaceous' compost.

Filling a bed or pot

Fill beds in layers, gently firming down each layer as you proceed. The soil will settle in the first six months and will need topping up occasionally. There is little point in mixing composts to your plant's requirements: commercial manufacturers prepare their blends with great care and are practised at achieving the correct nutritional balance.

For general use I usually recommend a multi-purpose peat-based compost. This will support a wide range of plant material and is well balanced and relatively light. If you need an even lighter compost, mix in no more than one part in five of horticultural vermiculite, or 'perlite'. Vermiculite has no nutritional value and the savings in weight

Above left On a wall or screen, many of the plants should be tied in at regular intervals. They should also be shaped carefully to prevent them becoming too rampant or swamping their neighbours.

Left The best planting schemes are planned taking the eventual size of species into account at the start. Even so, many plants will often need judicious thinning and sorting on an annual basis to keep them looking perfect.

Right Overcrowding can become a problem in small areas such as roof gardens and balconies, so take care when selecting plants, particularly when the view is as fine as this.

Above In this kind of paved area the tree pits will need to be deep and well prepared before planting is undertaken, and the trees will need regular irrigation while they are becoming established. The clipped hedges add immeasurably to this composition.

FILLING A POT WITH SOIL

Like beds and containers, pots should be free-draining to prevent waterlogging.

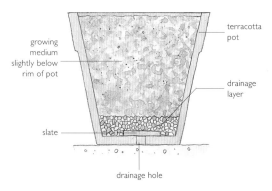

growing medium slightly below rim of pot

terracotta pot

drainage layer

slate

drainage hole

Above The drainage hole is covered with a piece of crock or slate, and the drainage medium and the pot filled with growing medium.

are minimal. It is almost certainly best to stick with a good multi-purpose compost but ensure that the weight of your garden is not in danger of exceeding the surface's load-bearing capacity.

Even the smallest pots can be filled with multi-purpose compost, but they still need a layer of drainage medium. This can be broken terracotta pots or 'crocks', or expanded clay granules. You can prevent the latter from dropping through the drainage hole in the bottom by covering the hole with a piece of crock, small stone or piece of slate. Standing pots on small 'feet' lifts them slightly clear of the surface. This helps drainage and the additional height gives slugs and snails a harder time if they try and reach the foliage above!

As compost tends to dry out quickly in a pot it can be useful to add a water-retentive gel to the mix. It swells when wet and holds water longer, so needs to be watered less frequently than the equivalent volume of compost. It can also be used in hanging baskets and window boxes. A planted bed will benefit from a 50–80mm (2–3in) thick mulch of medium-grade bark chips, which are heavy enough not to be blown away by a strong wind and help to retain moisture in the compost.

Rockwool

Using rockwool as a growing medium is a recent innovation which has its own advantages. It is relatively light, even when wet, since the slab needs to be only 100mm (4in) thick for average-sized container planting, or doubled over for larger plants and pots. It is placed over a membrane above a 50mm layer of expanded clay granules. Water is fed into the drainage layer at the bottom, where it is drawn upwards by the rockwool and roots. A drainage point to remove excess moisture is positioned at the top of the drainage layer.

Rockwool has no nutritional value, so after the first season when the plant has exhausted the nutrients placed within the rootball by the nurseryman, regular feeding is necessary. Mulching also helps to retain moisture. Rockwool products are usually only available through professional outlets and installation is normally carried out by specialist landscape companies.

Buying plants

Nearly all plants are now available from suppliers 'container-grown'. Unless the ground is water-logged, they can usually be planted at any time, except the hottest parts of summer or during the winter. Some plants are more difficult to propagate and grow than others, and this is reflected in their retail price, as is their age and size. You are often paying for the length of growing time.

Checking that plants are healthy

When you buy a plant you should always check that it looks healthy, has clean foliage and shows no obvious signs of disease. If you buy plants in autumn, which is an excellent planting time, don't be put off by foliage that is starting to drop from deciduous shrubs, or dying down in the case of hardy perennials. Look at the bottom of the container: it's a bad sign if the roots are forcing their way through holes in the pot; it means that the plant is root-bound and has almost certainly been on the shelf or in the bed for too long.

Above Climbers grow in different ways: some self-cling to a wall while others use tendrils, or simply lean against a support. Recognize this fact when planning the bed and buying the plants and make sure that the right kind of support is available.

Below As long as they are fed and watered on a regular basis, many plants are particularly successful in pots. Acers grow very well in pots and can be complemented with low ground cover, which will in turn help to retain moisture.

Above By training plants against a wall in a decorative fashion, you can make a virtue out of necessity of keeping them tidy. Tied in carefully, and clipped regularly, the plants will become a feature, with strong directional emphasis.

Above Even the most uncompromising situation, in deep shade and damp conditions, can be suitable for certain types of planting, as borne out by the obviously healthy condition of the ferns perched on this piece of stone.

Implementing a planting scheme

If you have prepared a planting scheme it may be sensible to implement it in stages if the area is relatively large. This will also help to spread the cost.

The beds should be freshly prepared and moist without being waterlogged. Working from the plan, lay the available plants out in their positions in the beds. At this stage you can easily make minor adjustments. Bear in mind that no two plants, even of the same type, are ever alike: this may mean that one side looks slightly better facing in one or another direction.

Planting technique

With multi-purpose compost you should need only a trowel for planting. Excavate the holes one at a time, before easing the plant from its container, taking care not to damage the roots and teasing out any that are starting to grow around the rootball. Try the plant in the hole, bearing in mind that the top of the rootball should end up at the same level as the surrounding soil, and adjust the excavation accordingly. Finally, firm the plant into the compost and water it in gently.

Above Plants such as vines are both productive and decorative, but to be at their very best they need regular pruning and tying in to a supporting structure.

Supporting larger plants and climbers

Larger shrubs or small trees may well need to be staked into the edges of beds or other structures. Professional landscapers sometimes use an underground guying system; tied in to the rootball.

Climbers should be tied back to a trellis or on horizontal wires. The cane that is initially in the rootball for additional support can be left in place until growth is under way. If planted against a building, climbers should be spaced 150–230mm (6–9in) from the wall to maximize the amount of rainfall they receive.

Bulbs

Bulbs should be planted at specific depths in the soil. If bulbs are 'blind' – that is, they do not flower – this is usually because they were planted too shallow. They should be planted at about four times the depth of the bulb which, for a daffodil, for example, is 15cm (6in). Always ensure that the bulbs sit snugly on the bottom of the excavated hole with no air gap. In heavy soil they often need a little sharp sand under them, but in multipurpose compost this should not be necessary.

POSITIONING A ROOTBALL IN SOIL

It is important that container-grown specimens are planted at the correct depth.

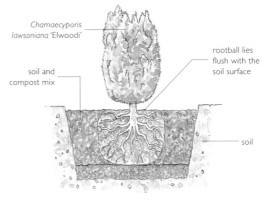

Above Make sure that the top of the rootball is level with the surrounding soil. This provides both stability and the best possible conditions for the roots.

GUYING A LARGE PLANT UNDER SOIL

Trees and larger shrubs may need extra support when grown in containers.

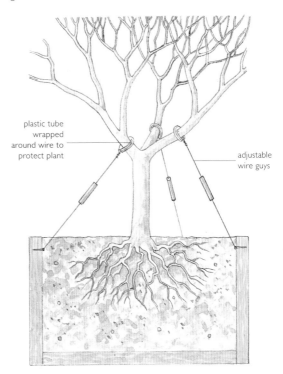

Above Large plants should by guyed into the sides of the container to prevent them blowing over or damaging their root systems by moving in the wind.

Maintenance
Annual and...

Work that must be done each year will include making good any damage to structural elements, repainting, pruning and cleaning. All this work is usually undertaken while the garden is dormant in winter but will help to prolong its summer beauty for many years.

...daily care

Daily work in the garden need not be a chore. When done regularly, tasks such as deadheading roses or watering your plants can be a very relaxing way to spend summer evenings and increase your enjoyment and appreciation of your garden.

Left Maintenance is, of course, an integral part of gardening, but if it is done regularly, the workload need not be heavy. By choosing low-maintenance plants and fittings, you can keep the work to an absolute minimum.

Hard landscape

The hard landscape of a garden includes all the structural elements: the fences, railings and trellis, decking, paving or tiling, planters and beds, walls, paintwork, railings, and furniture. In order to prolong the life of these items and to ensure that they look their best and remain safe, a certain amount of winter maintenance is also necessary. Of course, if anything becomes apparent during the course of the summer that might prove hazardous, more expensive to repair if left undone until the autumn, or might spoil the look of the garden, it should be dealt with immediately. There will also be some regular, more frequent work to be undertaken, such as clearing drains and gutters in the autumn, or checking the pond's pump filter. On the other hand, some more complicated work may not need to be carried out so often: for instance, if you are lucky, the walls and chimneys may only need repointing once every thirty years or so.

Above left Water can be a feature as well as a necessity in any garden. Both decorative items such as fountain heads and practical items such as taps will need descaling with a non-toxic solution or by scrubbing from time to time to prevent a build-up of lime.

Left The most elegant and sophisticated design situations can also require minimal maintenance. This garden is a delightful study in the juxtaposition of materials in what must be the ultimate in low-maintenance gardening.

Boundaries

Whether they are on a roof or at ground level, boundaries may be subject to the vagaries of climate and can sustain weathering and possible structural weakening, or damage by wind. The boundary railing is your ultimate safety barrier and must be checked at all points to ensure that its strength and stability is never compromised.

Timber

Timber is particularly susceptible to weathering and will need regular attention. Stained fences and screens should be brushed down and treated with a non-toxic preservative annually or less frequently, depending on their condition. Do not use creosote as it is poisonous to plants.

Any plants on the boundary should be taken down carefully before the woodwork is treated or painted. Attaching plants to the fence with horizontal strands of wire allows them to be released, then refixed when the job is finished.

Fixings such as posts, brackets and straining wires should be checked carefully and tightened or renewed as necessary. On a terrace at ground

Above Where storage space is limited, furniture may need to be left outside throughout the year. In this case it may have been chosen for ease of care or minimal maintenance.

level, damaged posts can be cut away just above the surface and bolted onto new concrete spurs, but on a roof the whole post should be replaced and firmly bolted in position.

As the wind is stronger at roof level than at ground level, wear can be correspondingly worse. Replace any structural elements with the best-quality materials possible: non-ferrous screws or nails will last longer than steel ones and pressure-treated timber will prove a better investment than untreated wood. In an ideal world, worn boards or other timber would be replaced using similar timber which is equally weathered. In practice, however, there is a danger that new timber will look glaringly obvious. If you don't want to wait for it to blend in, it can be aged artificially.

Overheads with closely spaced beams or those that are roofed with sheeting, should be cleaned regularly to remove leaves or other debris. Check that the screw fixings of canopies have not worn

123

TAKING DOWN TRAINED PLANTS

With forethought, it is possible to plan your garden so that your plants remain unharmed during any necessary maintenance to nearby structures.

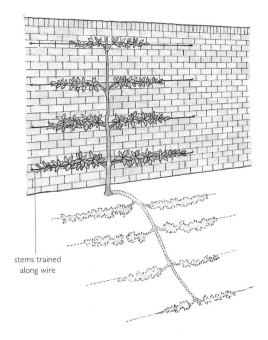

stems trained
along wire

Above If climbers are trained on wires they can be taken down, should the wall or fence need attention. The wires should be disconnected at either end and the plant lowered gently to the ground, ensuring that none of the branches are bent or strained. If you are doing anything with chemicals, make sure that you cover the plant until you have finished the job.

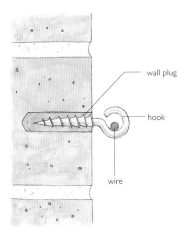

wall plug

hook

wire

Above Wires can be run through hooks that are screwed into wall plugs and simply lifted out as necessary.

or worked loose. Also check the framework of retractable awnings to ensure that all of the bolts and mountings are absolutely secure.

Painted metal

Painted metal fencing should be rubbed down and given a new coat. Plastic-coated surfaces can easily break down to expose the metal below which can then be liable to rust, so be sure to check for this problem.

Brickwork and rendering

Brickwork rarely needs attention, particularly if it is new, but check walls and chimney stacks where weathering may have weakened the mortar joints. Old brick chimneys can in extreme cases become dangerous: these should be removed or repaired urgently. Certainly removal, and even repointing, is best left to a professional, as it may involve scaffolding around a structure. Walls or raised beds that have been rendered will need to be repainted from time to time. If you have climbers trained on hinged trellis, this can be taken down as a unit to enable you to reach the wall behind. If the render does crack or break down it should be renewed before any blockwork below starts to deteriorate.

Glass panels

If the fixings of glass panels or screens become loose the panels could vibrate and finally break, so they should be checked regularly. They should either be cleaned with a detergent which does not harm plants, or else nearby plants should be removed while cleaning is in progress.

Floors

Decking, tiling, paving or other floor surfaces always receive a great deal of wear, but provided that the floor is well constructed and laid, maintenance should be minimal.

Drainage

Drainage channels and gullies should be cleaned regularly to avoid blockages. Standing water can quickly undermine the surface or, in roof gardens, leak into the rooms below. One of the advantages of decking made of removable panels is that these can be lifted for the removal of any leaves or litter. Drainage outlets or open joints in raised beds or containers should be accessible so that they can be checked and kept clear.

Paving and tiling

Any paved or tiled surfaces should be swept down regularly to remove dead leaves and other litter. If slippery green algae forms in shady areas, it can usually be removed by scrubbing with a stiff brush and detergent.

Removing and replacing individual paving modules is a delicate job on a roof, particularly if they have been mortared or fixed with mastic adhesive. Always be conscious of the waterproof membrane below: it may be better to leave it well alone if there is a likelihood of causing damage. Replacing any damaged paving in a terrace is straightforward as slabs, bricks or other modules can simply be chopped out and replaced.

Above This decorative tiling border is such a delicate and well-laid detail that is must be kept clean and properly maintained to be seen at its best.

Below While timber can be allowed to weather to an attractive finish, it nevertheless needs regular attention to prevent rot. Any damaged sections should be replaced immediately.

PREVENTING A POND FROM FREEZING OVER

A pond that supports fish or wildlife should never be allowed to freeze over in winter.

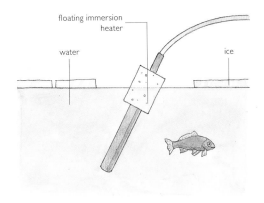

Above A small floating immersion heater will keep a circle of water ice free. It should not be allowed to touch the side of the pond.

Above Any open area of water, whether a swimming pool or a pond, needs to be kept clean. Leaves in particular can be caught in a net and removed once surrounding trees are clear. Pump filters should be cleaned regularly and any electrical fittings checked and, if necessary, repaired professionally.

Decking

Decks should be regularly checked for the safety of all components, particularly where they are built out over steep slopes. The railings and fixings close to ground level are perhaps the most important. The junction between posts and concrete pads, or where posts are bedded directly into soil, must be regularly checked. The timber should be treated with non-toxic preservatives and any damaged or weak components should be replaced immediately.

Beds, pots and containers

Timber raised beds should be checked inside and out for rot. Fibreglass inserts should prevent any internal damage, but if the beds have been lined with polythene there could be leakage and subsequent deterioration. Individual boards may need to be replaced or sections pieced in. Applications of preservative or paint should be carried out as for other surfaces in the garden: if this is done regularly, the beds should last for many years. Pots and containers should be examined annually and any made from timber treated as above. Since some terracotta is not frost proof and can flake or shatter in freezing conditions, these items should be brought inside or placed under cover away from the frost during winter.

Built-in furniture

Built-in furniture should be treated as for other timber features in the garden, but free-standing furniture should be rubbed down annually and teak oil or a proprietary preservative should be applied. Wrought iron or alloy furniture can be rubbed down, primed and painted, while plastics should be washed with detergent to remove algae, particularly if the items are left out all year.

Water features

Well-designed water features need relatively little maintenance. Leaves left in the water can cause toxins to build up in pools at ground level, but this is usually less of a problem on a roof. If leaves do fall in the area, it is easy enough to place a fine-mesh plastic net over the surface in autumn,

removing it with the leaves once the main drop is over. The bottom of the pool can be cleaned out from time to time, but only if there is a significant accumulation of debris. It should not be necessary to drain and refill the pool as this would destroy the natural balance which has taken time to develop. If necessary, drain about a quarter of the water and replenish with new water.

Pump filters should be cleaned regularly and electric cables and fittings checked. If there is any sign of damage, switch off the equipment immediately and seek professional help.

If a pool is allowed to freeze over in winter, toxic gases will quickly build up and these can be harmful or even fatal to fish. A small pool immersion heater will keep an area clear (*see p. 126*), or you can float a rigid inflatable ball on the surface to maintain a hole in the ice. Do not crack the ice with a hammer or other heavy object as the shock waves can stun any creatures in the pool.

Millstones, cobbles and boulders or similar small water features should need little attention except topping up in warm weather. Cables and pumps should be checked regularly. Limescale can slowly build up on water spouts. This should be carefully scraped away, as it could eventually block the flow or throw it off-centre.

Electric cables

Electricity is perfectly safe in a garden when it is installed and maintained correctly. Faults, particularly when water is present, are potentially fatal, so lighting and power circuits should be kept separate and should run through automatic circuit breakers. Installation and remedial work should be left to a qualified electrician, but always check the condition of cables and fittings, and take care when cultivating beds where lighting is installed.

Irrigation

Limescale should be removed from any drip-feed hoses or nozzles. Hoses should be checked periodically for splits or signs of perishing. Drip-feed systems should also be adjusted as plants grow and spread.

Soft landscape

The growth patterns of plants on a roof or within the confines of a raised bed or container are different from those of plants in the open garden. This means that some aspects of their maintenance are different. On a roof or balcony, the winds may be stronger and large plants and climbers may need to be supported on stakes or tied back to the wall or to trellis. Plants that are grown in containers are also dependent on the gardener for the majority of their water and all of their food and rarely grow to the full size indicated in catalogues or at the garden centre.

Support

Stakes can often be neatly screwed to surrounding timberwork. Any ties and supports should be regularly checked and adapted as plants develop. Shrubs, too, may also benefit from some support. Using the correct plastic ties is essential: avoid wire, string, cord or anything that may cut into the stem or trunk. Garden ties can be obtained from any good garden centre or landscaper.

Feeding

What, when and how much plants should be fed depends on the type of plants involved and the containers in which they are grown. Initially it is worth understanding what kinds of fertilizers are available and their characteristics.

All plant material needs food and once it has been consumed or washed out of the soil it needs to be replaced in some way. Some kinds of plants also need a specific level of acidity or alkalinity to take up nutrients effectively. Ericaceous plants such as rhododendron, azalea and heather thrive in an acid soil (one with a low pH value) and so should be grown in an ericaceous compost which may well contain peat or another acidifier.

Fertilizers

Fertilizers can be broadly categorized as quick acting, steady release and slow release. There are also different methods of application: powders or granules can be worked into the soil when planting or applied as a top dressing sprinkled around plants; liquid forms can be used as a foliar feed sprayed or watered onto leaves or watered in over

Above left The different ways that plants can be grown include pots or containers or in the open ground. In addition, they can be either free-standing or supported against a wall or fence.

Left Climbers can be tied back to trellis or by horizontal strands of wire. Attaching them to wires can be a slightly easier prospect for maintenance, as well as less visually intrusive.

Right Plants can also be used to support each other. Here, some of the tendrils of the clematis have wound themselves up through the tall, erect shrub behind.

Above Bulbs and annual bedding plants can provide instant colour and are particularly useful in a new garden while slower-growing material is knitting together.

the root system. Soil conditioners and mulches also add some nutrition to soil, but fertility should be boosted by other means from time to time.

Container-grown plants will contain a slow-release fertilizer incorporated by the nurseryman. This fertilizer can often be seen as small round granules on the surface of the rootball.

Shrubs and trees will benefit from steady- or slow-release fertilizers. However, steady-release types give up their nutrition faster in hot conditions, such as those often found on a roof garden, and may need to be supplemented with a liquid feed during the growing season.

Annual planting, including half-hardy bedding plants, will respond to liquid feeds around the roots and foliar feed through the leaves, while hardy perennials, or herbaceous plants, can be fed with both steady-release and liquid feeds. Bulbs benefit from a slow-release type such as bonemeal, which can be incorporated into the soil or compost in the autumn so that it is available when the bulbs need it in the spring.

How much food?

Avoid the temptation to over-feed plants, as it can cause scorching and even death. Always read the directions carefully and follow them to the letter. All garden chemicals should be kept in a locked cupboard, safely out of children's reach.

Certain sophisticated irrigation systems have the facility to incorporate a liquid feed and distribute it to plants automatically, but again the balance is critical: plants must not be over-fed.

Mulches are useful, particularly on a roof garden, to retain moisture. If sufficiently heavy they will also prevent lightweight compost being blown away. All organic mulches degrade over a period of time, rotting down to add a little nutrition and structure to the growing medium, so they need topping up on an annual or biannual basis.

Plants grown in rockwool will survive for two years on the slow-release fertilizer already in the rootball. From then on, a steady-release fertilizer should be added to maintain fertility, as well as liquid feed if necessary.

Annual maintenance

Some shrubs simply need to be pruned once each year to keep them neat and tidy, whereas others require a specific amount of pruning at a specific time of year to enable them to flower in following years; however, some shrubs need virtually no pruning at all. Herbaceous plants should be lifted

Above If you wish to grow food crops – such as apples, pears and citrus fruits – both in containers and on plants that last from year to year, regular feeding will be essential to maintain good yields.

Right As a general rule, the larger the pot, the happier a plant will be, revelling in having ample room for its roots. It also has the benefit for you that it will need to be watered less often. Even so, you should watch for extremes of weather, which can be detrimental.

Above left and above Plants can be trained to produce a formal or informal result. Large-leafed plants, with a sprawling habit, look best trained to ramble. Smaller-leaved plants with more compact habits can be encouraged into a controlled shape, such as an arch.

and divided, which produces more plants if you need them, or more attractive ones if you discard the older, less healthy parts. On the other hand, bulbs grown in containers need a little more care than those which are simply left in the ground in a larger garden.

Pruning shrubs

The pruning of shrubs, as distinct from the day-to-day deadheading and tidying of plants, is generally carried out on an annual basis. Many shrubs need little or no attention apart from the occasional removal of dead, weak or diseased wood. The practice of shearing over plants should be avoided, since it produces an artificial shape and can remove flowering wood. Shrubs which need to be pruned to keep them flowering at their best can be divided into separate categories.

Spring- and early-flowering deciduous shrubs that flower on stems developed in the previous season should be pruned immediately after they have flowered. The flowering stems should be cut back by about a third to strong lateral shoots. The resulting shape should be balanced since the plant

will now produce new shoots that will flower the following year. Shrubs typical of this group include *Weigela*, *Philadelphus*, lilac and *Deutzia*.

Established shrubs that flower in late summer such as *Buddleia davidii*, *Lavatera* and *Perovskia* should be cut back in early spring to within two or three buds of the old wood to allow new wood to develop. The last group includes *Cornus* (dog wood), shrubby willows and elders. The first two have coloured stems that look superb in winter. The stem colour is strongest on the current season's wood: if the stems are pruned hard in early spring, they will grow through the summer and look at their best the following winter.

Climbers

As they give vertical cover, climbers are among the most useful plants on a roof garden, although they are untidy if left unpruned. The rules are generally the same as for shrubs: old wood on spring-flowering types should be cut back by about a third.

Wisteria, which is such a popular spring-flowering plant, should be pruned twice in the same year. In midsummer the side shoots can be cut back to within six leaves of the main stems and then during the following winter these same stems can be cut hard back to within three buds.

Passion flower, which flowers relatively late, can have its side shoots pruned back nearly to the main stems in spring, while honeysuckle can have some of the older stems cut out after flowering.

Some tender climbers can be successful in relatively mild rooftop conditions, but if you grow them it is best to remove frost-damaged shoots in spring, since these can die back and become infected with disease.

Clematis is another justly popular climber, but the rules for pruning it can be confusing, as pruning times vary according to when the flowering shoots develop. The real problem is that if you don't prune, the new growth which produces all the flower occurs progressively higher and farther from the base, leaving unsightly bare stems below. There are three major groups of clematis: those that flower before midsummer on the previous season's wood; those that flower in late spring or early summer and then come into bloom again in late summer; and finally, those that flower in late summer and early autumn on wood grown in that season. Examples of the early-flowering types are the popular *C. montana* and the wonderful blue *C. macropetala*, as well as the various *C. alpina*.

If you have sufficient room, vigorous varieties of the first group can be left unpruned and simply clipped back with shears after flowering. If you want to keep them really neat, then train them onto a framework straight from planting and cut all the flowering shoots back to a strong bud at the base in early summer.

Right Climbing and rambling roses will quickly form a tangle if not tied in and selectively thinned. Any training is best started when the plant is young and not left until it is mature.

Above Pots and containers do, of course, need regular irrigation, and this is best carried out in the early morning or in the evening, when the sun is not strong enough to scorch their foliage.

Above Provided that there is enough of the correct growing medium, there are few limits to what you can grow on a roof. Here, a virtual meadow has been created with succulent plants. Once established this kind of plant grouping will require very little maintenance and is ideal for carpeting large areas.

Those clematis that flower twice in the same season, such as *C.* 'Nellie Moser' and *C.* 'The President', should have between a quarter and a third of their stems cut back in late winter to the highest pair of strong buds. After the first flowering, cut back another quarter of the stems to produce flower early the next year. The last group, which includes *C. tangutica*, *C. viticella*, *C.* 'Jackmanii', *C.* 'Ernest Markham' and *C.* 'Hagley Hybrid', is easy to care for: cut each stem back in late winter to the lowest pair of well-developed buds. The new growth of clematis is brittle and should be tied back carefully in order to avoid wind damage.

Dividing herbaceous plants

Most herbaceous plants (or hardy perennials) should be lifted and divided roughly every three years in early autumn or mid-spring when the soil is warm enough to encourage root development. Lift the plants and then either carefully prise the rooted sections apart by hand or using two small border forks placed back to back. If the central section of the plant has become hard and woody, producing little growth, it can be cut out and discarded. Replant the new sections with a little steady-release fertilizer.

Bulbs

Bulbs that have been naturalized in raised beds should be allowed to die down naturally after they have flowered. Do not be tempted to cut off the green foliage before it goes brown. If you have bulbs grown in pots and containers, they too should be allowed to die down before being carefully lifted. The leaves should be cut off and the bulbs then stored in a dry, dark place to be replanted the following autumn.

Aquatic plants

Most aquatic plants die down in winter and if the situation is not too windy the brown foliage can be left in place to provide extra interest. If the foliage does get blown flat, it should be removed. Replanting aquatic plants is best done in late spring when the warmer water will encourage new growth.

Day-to-day maintenance

Day-to-day jobs become second nature to most gardeners and include deadheading spent blooms to sustain flowering, supporting hardy perennials as they grow, and tying in climbers. Such work is hardly time consuming and can again be enormously satisfying and restful.

Pests and diseases

Something else to keep a look out for is disease and insect attack, which can happen at virtually any time of the growing season. Blackfly, greenfly (aphids), caterpillars, and slugs and snails can be prevented with chemicals which should always be used according to the instructions. If you prefer not to use chemicals – I try to avoid them – there are a number of biological controls available, such as nematodes. Make sure that chemicals are stored under lock and key, away from children.

Disease is usually a viral or fungal attack of some kind such as black spot on roses, or mildew. Part of the solution is to ensure that plants are watered and fed correctly as disease can strike more easily if the plants are under-nourished or under stress. Again there are chemical treatments which are normally successful if they are applied early enough and exactly as directed.

Plants which are thriving in their growing conditions are generally far more resistant to pests and diseases than material that has to battle for existence. In my own garden I have little time to pamper plants and as a result I choose things which enjoy life rather than struggle for it, allowing me to do the same with my garden.

Irrigation and watering

All plants need water, although some species are more tolerant than others of the dry conditions on a roof, balcony or raised bed at ground level.

Irrigation systems range from simple hand-held devices to complex computer-driven systems that function under any conditions, whether you are home or not. All automatic irrigation works on the same principal, that of delivering the water almost directly to the roots of the plants. Watering should be carried out regularly and in the heat of summer, early in the morning, and in the evening to prevent leaf scorch and conserve water.

LOCALIZED IRRIGATION

Irrigation systems can remove the need for watering cans.

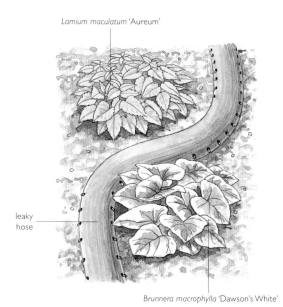

Lamium maculatum 'Aureum'

leaky hose

Brunnera macrophylla 'Dawson's White'

Above 'Leaky' pipe systems allow water to ooze around plants.

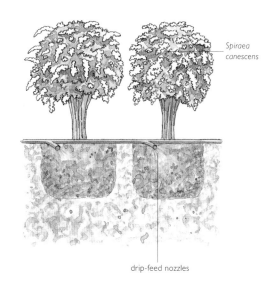

Spiraea canescens

drip-feed nozzles

Above Drip-feed irrigation ensures that water goes to the roots.

Accessories

Selecting...

The way in which your accessories are chosen and used is as important as the overall design: make sure that the design has a direct influence over the style of ornaments that you use.

...and positioning

Larger ornamental features should be put in place after the main structure of the garden or area of it has been laid out, but before the plants. There are no unbreakable rules, provided that an item is sited in keeping with the scale of its immediate surroundings.

Left Some pots are far too beautiful to plant up and rely on their sculptural outline for effect. A combination of planted and unplanted pots can be positioned to great effect in the garden.

Focal points

Major features such as water, statuary, urns and obelisks can be used to draw the eye and as important focal points in the overall composition. Think about them in detail while you are preparing the design as they will be permanent or semi-permanent parts of it, although I feel strongly that they should be moved from time to time. Features can give directional emphasis, be the focus of a vista on a long balcony or provide the sight and sound of water on a split-level terrace. They will be the punctuation marks of the garden, and so should be used sparingly.

Positioning and choice

An important initial consideration on a roof or balcony is the weight of any ornamental feature. If you are concerned about this, check your initial survey to see which parts are strong enough.

A wide range of synthetic materials is used to mimic traditional ones while still remaining lightweight. Fibreglass containers are manufactured to look like lead or terracotta, and it is becoming more difficult to tell the real thing, although there is an aesthetic argument against this use of synthetics to copy traditional materials. Plastics and synthetics are fluid, malleable materials which offer the chance of dramatic, contemporary and colourful shapes. Stone, terracotta and lead tend to be used in more traditional work, although they too can be featured in stunningly fresh ways.

Water features

Water is a significant element in any garden, in whatever position and whatever guise. It provides a feeling of movement, a cooling influence on a

Above left Sculpture comes in all shapes and sizes, alive as well as inert. Topiary is a fascinating art form: in this case, creeping plants are grown over a frame to create a fairground horse, creating a dramatic focal point.

Left Water is always both visually and aurally interesting. Although a grand feature like this entails considerable constructional skills, the end result is dramatic.

Above Even the tiniest bubble fountain can create a focal point in an intimate situation, such as a balcony. It really is all a matter of scale and positioning.

hot summer's day and, of course, a background sound which can be enormously soothing.

Small water features are often traditional in design. They vary from diminutive wall-mounted bowls with water cascading from one to another, to lion or fish heads that gush into a pool below.

On a contemporary note, you can buy rather more complicated, but still attractive, millstone or boulder features. The latter can be built within a raised area, possibly surrounded by planting, to provide a delightful focal point. Water is pumped

Above At first sight this appears to be a stunningly beautiful piece of free-standing sculpture, but if you look very closely you will see that it is, in fact, a water feature attached to a mirror.

Above Which came first, the gazebo or the framing columns? In any case the combination produces pure drama set against a rugged landscape. Keeping the balustrade clear of pots and planting might have heightened the focus onto the gazebo even further.

from a tank to play over the visible top surface. This can either be in natural or synthetic materials, which are often far lighter. These need not be imitations of natural materials: I have recently designed acrylic mirror pyramids of varying sizes which are a variation on this theme. Water is pumped from the sump to the top of the feature where it bubbles out to slide down over the sides and then back into the sump. The ever-changing reflections are fascinating. Variations on a watery theme are endless: found objects, pots, copper fish, barrels, glazed bowls and mini pools can all be incorporated into designs. They are also safer for children than areas of open water.

Water also attracts wildlife. Birds drink and bathe at most features while fish, dragon- and damselflies will breed and hatch in a larger, well balanced pool. A roof garden with water and plants can be a rich wildlife habitat anywhere.

Ornaments

Garden ornaments should not be used merely to dress up a garden: they should become part of it, as points of emphasis, interest or fun. The fun element is too often forgotten. Some people regard garden gnomes as icons of bad taste, but other animals and figures can be well modelled and add to a composition. If you like a piece and have a place for it, use it; it is, after all, your garden.

Sculpture

There are many classical statues to choose from, ranging from poor renditions in badly cast concrete through faithful replicas in reconstructed stone to original works of art. Prices vary, and an original piece could cost more than the entire garden. Size and, especially where conventional materials are used, weight can also vary greatly.

There are few good contemporary designs available and it is almost impossible to find these through a garden centre or shop. This is not for a lack of sculptors but rather from a lack of interest or of awareness on the part of the public. Good examples can sometimes be found at big garden shows, but because they are often especially made for the show the prices are high. Individual items are produced in a wide range of materials including wood, various metals – some of which are lightweight – bent wire, glass and acrylics. While the prices reflect the originality of the piece, genuine works of art do have investment value.

Scale is another important factor to consider. A relatively large piece may look correct in a garden at ground level, but in the smaller area of a roof or balcony could be out of place. Look at the space and choose carefully. Bear in mind also that the bigger the piece the more it will draw the eye and appear to diminish the surrounding space, so larger items should be sited particularly carefully.

Urns

Urns are usually large, often handsome classical pots that can be used as ornaments without the addition of planting, raised on plinths to increase their visual impact. Used singly they become focal points, but in pairs, to either side of a doorway or other feature, they focus the viewer's attention on

Above Just occasionally you can build something that is both unusual and has great charm. There is enormous power in this large pot built entirely from thin pieces of slate.

Below Because they can have personal associations that no one else would understand, items such as sculpture are best bought by the owner of the garden rather than the designer or architect.

the central object, so increasing tension as you approach. Classical examples are appropriate to a traditional garden design, although they can be used with panache alongside post-modern architecture. Many urns are suitable for interiors as well as outside and this creates an obvious opportunity for linkage, particularly if there is planting on both sides of the divide.

Terracotta

Terracotta is a popular material for ornaments, but in an exposed site, perhaps on a terrace at ground level, it should be checked for frost resistance. Because terracotta is clay-based, the modelling can be more detailed and sharper than on reconstituted stone. As it can be cast more thinly, a terracotta item is almost always lighter than a similar one in stone. It is usually a reddish brown, but the cream form – faience – can look superb in the right setting.

Obelisks

Obelisks draw the eye and act as punctuation marks in any setting: they can introduce a point of drama used either singly or in pairs. In a small space they should be proportionally small.

Other ornaments

These can include bird baths, sundials, boulders or 'found objects'. Many are intensely personal objects, and for this reason I very rarely choose these items for clients. You should use your imagination, both in the acquisition and the siting of such objects, and your garden will be richer for it.

In small areas, walls and screens can hold a wide range of ornaments, from classical plaques to various works in relief. Planters and baskets can add life and colour, while paintings, either directly on the wall or on a wide variety of materials, can be placed singly or as compositions.

Left and right The human figure is a popular subject for sculpture. Here the treatments of two classical figures are different: the modern setting sets off the vigour of the statue on the left, whereas the plant niche emphasizes the peaceful nature of the statue on the right.

Furniture

Garden furniture can be most uncomfortable. The golden rule is to try it out before you buy – sit on a chair for five minutes and check whether your knees fit comfortably under the table and don't be seduced by what looks attractive in the shop. Gardens are all about relaxation, and if you are not comfortable, you will not be able to relax. There are myriad styles and patterns, in a wide range of materials, including metal, plastic and timber. The key is to pick a style that complements that of the area and then to find a comfortable, practical example.

Materials

Which material or combination of materials you choose depends on a number of factors. Is the weather routinely good enough for you to leave your furniture out all year? Will you want to move it regularly? Do you mind hot plastic or cold metal? Is your garden going to be 'modern' or 'classical' in style? Does the furniture need to be hard-wearing enough for children?

Timber

Timber furniture is the most widely available, and styles in it range from the pure classicism of a 'Lutyens' bench that will stand alone as a superb focal point, to a homely, well designed and inexpensive set that will look good in most situations. As with most other things in the garden, it is important to keep furniture simple.

Most good, durable designs are made from hardwoods, which last longer than the softer pine. Some hardwoods are taken from non-renewable rain forest, so check before you buy that the timber comes from a properly managed resource.

Furniture on a roof garden or balcony may have to stand outside all year for lack of storage space, so bare timber will need to be maintained by using a 'teak' or other preservative oil on an annual basis. Painted furniture will need to be rubbed down and repainted from time to time.

Where space is at a premium, furniture sets that are either folding or that stack closely together can be invaluable, and free-standing loungers can be wonderful for quiet relaxation during the heat of the summer. To maximize your floor space, these can often be neatly and securely hung on a wall when they are not being used.

Above left The most important point about garden furniture is that it should be both comfortable and blend with its setting.

Left A modern roof garden deserves modern, bold furniture. Here, the curves of these metal and cloth chairs highlight the angularity and strong lines of the framework.

Right This built-in seating not only forms an integral part of the layout of the garden, it is also an effective way of adding colour.

Plastic

Not very long ago nearly all plastic furniture was considered to be cheap and nasty and the only colour available was white. There is now an enormous range of well-designed lightweight items in a huge range of colours and combinations. White is in fact a poor choice on a roof, as the glare can be almost intolerable.

One of the advantages of plastic furniture is that it can be allowed to stand outside all year. Loose covers can be brought inside, washed and stored at the onset of winter.

Metal

Metal furniture can be very uncomfortable to sit on. Many copies of traditional wrought iron or bent wire patterns are unusable for more than a few minutes. Again, do test furniture before you buy it. Some examples are, of course, perfectly comfortable to sit on or lounge in. Many of these are contemporary designs in a combination of metal and synthetics, both of which are usually extremely durable. Light tubular alloy is convenient and is also often used.

On a more traditional note, park bench styles of iron with timber slats can look and feel particularly good: excellent reproductions are available.

Fabric

Fabric furniture comes in a variety of styles; my own favourite is the traditional deck chair. The folding wooden frames can be hung with the fabric of your choice, possibly one which echoes an interior colour scheme or pattern. Close relations are 'directors' chairs, which are nearly as comfortable and also fold up for easy storage.

Hammocks are another popular choice. They can be slung between any two secure fixings, although the strength of all the fixings should be checked regularly. On a roof or balcony there is often the opportunity to fix stout eyes into a wall and the hammock folds away when not in use. Hammocks with an integral frame are usually a little too large and cumbersome for a small area.

Bean bags are popular with young, old and pets alike. They are ideal for an additional influx of friends and are extremely comfortable – just try to get a dog out of one! There are waterproof materials now available so that the bags can be left in a shower of rain without going soggy.

Overheads and awnings

Awnings, shades and parasols are particularly useful on a roof or balcony where the light values are often higher and shade is scarce. Awnings are normally fixed to the building and can be unreeled from a housing or let down from a folded position. They usually cast soft shade, as the light is filtered rather than cut out altogether, and the many colours and patterns can link with the fabrics and cushions used elsewhere. Fixings should be secure, with no risk of the blind or awning unravelling in a high wind.

Parasols have become increasingly popular over recent years and are available in a range of sizes. Some just span a table, others are large enough to cover a complete terrace or balcony. Secure fixing is again vital on a roof: parasols are really suitable for use only on calm days. Plain colours are often best for a large area, although vibrant colours can form a focal point.

At ground level, on a terrace, an informal awning can be made that creates a pool of wel-

come shadow by casting a sheet over the top of beams, or even over the low branches of a tree. The edges of the awning can be simply tied down and removed once the need for it is over. Scatter large cushions or bean bags underneath to complete the effect.

Above People rarely seem to take cushions into the garden, which is a shame, as they not only make garden furniture a good deal more comfortable, but they can extend a colour scheme from inside to outside.

HOW TO FIX A HAMMOCK

A hammock can be an ideal form of seating in limited space as it can be put away easily when it is not in use, thereby avoiding using unnecessary floor space.

Above Wooden furniture is durable and looks at home in most garden settings. It is immensely adaptable and is available in both traditional and modern styles to suit any garden design. Regular maintenance will ensure long life.

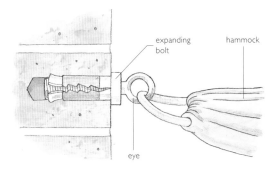

Above Hammocks are one of the most comfortable forms of garden furnishings, but need firm anchor points to ensure safety. Expanding bolts set into masonry are virtually indestructible, although the lashings should be checked on a regular basis.

Lighting

Lighting can be used to transform the feel of a garden or outside living space, extending the length of time for which it can be used each day and bringing a different dimension to every aspect of its composition. It is only recently that specialist companies and consultants have begun to offer their services in the area of lighting garden areas and, so far, few schemes have been any more adventurous than having basic floodlights fitted to ground spikes. You can, however, achieve sensitive and dramatic effects by installing practical and decorative forms in such a way that they can be revised as the garden develops and the plants grow.

Above left Lighting can be functional, decorative, or a combination of both. If fittings are visible, they should be selected to match the adjoining architecture or garden style.

Left Drama is an essential part of lighting design and here the soft glow brings surrealism to the strongly clipped shapes, as well as clearly illuminating the steps.

Above Lighting set close to the wall and shining upwards 'grazes' the surface, highlighting the wall and throwing the arch into relief.

Utility lighting

First the utility lighting should be positioned. As well as lighting hazards, it also acts as a crime deterrent, although halogen floodlights can often leave pools of shadow. It can pay to have a system which effectively illuminates the area when you need it to, or you can programme it into a timer.

The obvious areas for illumination include doorways or French windows, any changes of level and steps, as well as the main routes around the area and its features. A soft floodlight system will provide an ideal working spread and can be positioned where it is needed most. This need not be at a high level: you seldom need to light the top of your head, so fittings should be recessed alongside steps or doorways to illuminate where you are going walk or what you might walk into, such as uprights for overheads and other structures, which can be nearly invisible if painted black. A gentle light at the top or bottom, shining up or down, will be delicate and practical.

Utility lighting usually has a visible source, so fittings should blend in with the area. Imitation coach lamps look ostentatious on a contemporary façade, as can cast-iron street lamps. Remember that the light is more important than the fitting. Something straightforward will probably be less expensive than an ornate reproduction. However, some fittings are striking as works of art; they are expensive but also a tempting buy.

Decorative lighting

In decorative lighting schemes, the illumination takes precedence and the fittings should be invisible. Subtlety is better than a garish display: this is a good example of 'less is more'. The approach to garden illumination is similar to that for other elements of garden design: a composition where the whole is immediately obvious is less interesting than one containing surprises or different areas. The parts and features of the garden should be brought to life in darkness and displayed differently from the way they appear during the day.

Colour

Many garden centres sell every colour of light bulb, which can lead to unfortunate results. Red and orange turn plants a sickly hue, while green tends to wash foliage out completely. It is best usually to have a simple white or blue light; blue often has the effect of sharpening colour.

Spotlighting

Perhaps the best-known form of garden lighting is where a relatively concentrated beam is thrown onto a single object, usually a focal point, thereby throwing it into sharp relief. The question of

height is an important one: a beam should be sited so that you do not cross it in walking around the space. The fitting should be concealed, comparatively high-powered, and set some way away from the feature. This dramatic technique should be used sparingly – too many spotlights might look overpowering.

Uplighting and downlighting

These involve lights that are positioned at the top or bottom of a feature such as a classical column, pergola, statue or tree. The aim of the effect is to highlight the feature alone, rather than to light the immediate area.

Below Lighting effects can be created with lanterns and candles, as they flicker with far more character than electricity. The source may be weaker, but you can quickly adapt to the lower light value.

Floodlighting

Here the beam is more diffused to give a pool of illumination far wider and softer than a spotlight. The source can be relatively close, but again should be concealed. The technique is a general rather than a specific one and can be used to light a group of plants, pots or another feature. The edges fade out into the surrounding darkness.

Grazing light

This fabulous technique places floodlights at the top or bottom of a wall so that the light skims or 'grazes' the surface, picking up surface detail. It allows any relief to be emphasized by shadows running away from the light source and can be used to enormous effect on a roof garden, where walls or chimney stacks above can be brought into the composition.

Moonlighting

This is my own favourite decorative lighting system and entails siting a relatively low-powered floodlight in the branches of a tree, or just above the slats of overheads, so that the pattern of the structure and branches moving in the wind are cast on the ground below. The effect can be magical, particularly when seen from inside the house, looking out through large windows.

Backlighting

This is the opposite of floodlighting. A light is set close behind a feature to throw it into sharp relief. The feature could be a specific focal point, such as a statue or other ornament. A screen or trellis clothed with planting can also look superb, its shadows thrown onto an opposite wall.

Water

Lighting techniques should be kept simple in relation to water features. Floating, rotating, multi-coloured lights do little to enhance the tranquil mystery of a garden feature. Underwater lights should be white or blue. The object can be simply lit to have a gently diffused glow from beneath the surface, or something rather more specific, possibly by backlighting a cascade or statue.

Above Uplighters, carefully set nearly flush with the paving, form the perfect illumination to highlight this simple modern setting of multi-coloured, polished stone columns.

Installing lighting

As far as the installation is concerned, you should always employ professionals. If mains voltage is used they will bury the cables or install armoured cable and waterproofed switch gear. Much garden lighting works on a low voltage system, wired back to a transformer and circuit breaker in the house. If cables are laid on the surface, care will be needed when you are digging or trowelling. The advantage of such a method is that it can be easily adjusted. Schemes are best set up by two people: one to move the fittings around, the other to direct operations.

The future

Most garden lighting is still fairly conservative, but some designers have experimented with lasers, fibre optics and holograms. The results with lasers (which should be installed by experts) can be both stunning and beautiful. Fibre optics, which are safer as light is transmitted down the fibre rather than power, can also look delightful.

Special effects

In a small area, especially, special effects such as trompe-l'oeil and murals can provide a feeling of greater space. In truth they rarely fool anyone, at least after the first glance, but they are fun and that in itself is a good reason to employ them. Trompe-l'oeil and the clever use of mirrors are particularly valuable in small spaces, as they can make the area appear larger. Although trompe-l'oeil and mirrors used to deceive the eye are simply a piece of fun, they still need to be planned carefully to ensure that they work correctly: otherwise they will simply fall flat like a

joke with a poor punchline. Decorative trellis is another way of using creatively what is essentially a practical garden structure. It can be decoratively shaped, or coloured, or both. Even black-painted trellis has a quite different effect from that of a natural brown. Do bear in mind, however, that whatever special effect you choose should complement the style and feel of the rest of the garden.

Above left Visual trickery has been one of the designer's arts since time immemorial and should not be taken too seriously. Humour is an essential part of any garden composition.

Left This trompe-l'oeil is gloriously outrageous. It fools no-one but offers great charm and makes a real talking point. To make such compositions more effective they should, of course, be in the same style as the rest of the garden.

Trompe-l'oeil

Obviously trompe l'oeil involves trickery. The 'perspective' trellis with a central statue has become a cliché: there are more subtle ways of using the technique. A trellis 'window' with a view painted on the wall behind can be realistic and evocative, particularly if based on a romantic holiday vista. I have seen all sorts of permutations, from Mediterranean harbour views to a glimpse of a church spire and surrounding roofs.

Another version of trompe l'oeil that often works well uses a mirror instead of a statue inside a frame. The secret, when using mirrors in a garden to increase a feeling of space, is to ensure that they are angled so that you don't see yourself in them. They should be angled off into an area of planting so that it looks as though there is a new garden beyond. You can extend this trick by building a false arch or doorway; one of the best and most convincing I have seen involved a partially open false door with a mirror behind.

Mirrors can also be used in combination with water; behind a waterfall or within an arch with water flowing out in front. In both instances it looks as if the stream recedes back indefinitely. Another trick is to line the bottom of a very shallow pool with a mirror, which can make the water look far deeper. This could be invaluable on a roof garden. Some people are concerned about the possibility of birds flying into a reflective surface. I have found that the problem rarely arises as long as you partially cover the mirror with vegetation; this also enhances the illusory effect.

Decorative trellis

Trellis has been used in gardens as a divider and decorative element for hundreds of years. It has of late had something of a revival, but in classical rather than contemporary terms. As a result a wide range of classically inspired styles is available at most good garden centres. Alternatively, you

Right This delicate trellis provides a subtle backdrop to the more immediate action in front. The slats have the effect of breaking the light down, producing a real visual rhythm.

TYPES OF DECORATIVE TRELLIS

There are many different designs for trellises.

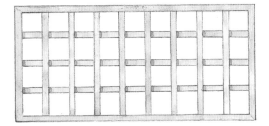

squares

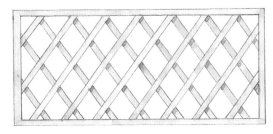

diamonds

doubled diamonds

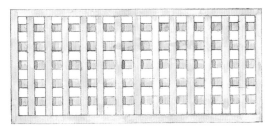

close squares

can have a specific design made to suit your own ideas and to fit a particular space. Basic patterns are normally based on squares or diamonds. Even so there is ample opportunity for variation in the detailing of posts and grouping and positioning of panels. Panels can have shapes cut out of them in a variation of the circular moongate principle, used at ground level to pierce a wall and allow a view into the landscape or next garden 'room'.

Above Mirrors can be enormously useful for increasing apparent visual space in a small garden. They need to be positioned carefully so that you cannot see yourself when you are walking towards them from the usual approach point.

While many people think of trellis in traditional terms, you can have a great deal of fun working in a more up-to-date style. Experiment with the positive and negative aspects of the material, cutting a pattern out of a run (a negative shape), or creating a pattern from the overall shape of the trellis, such as a tree or cloud (a positive shape). There are enormous possibilities since you can create virtually any shape or pattern ranging from regular cut outs running along a trellis, to a montage of shapes built up into a mural. As trellis is an ideal support for climbing plants, this adds to the fun. A climber could scramble up a trellis 'tree' or fill carefully shaped gaps. Pots grouped along a wall, beneath sections of a montage, could add to the effect. A striking composition, that I saw in the Far East, used clipped trees which precisely filled the shapes cut out of a long, complex run of trellis. At first it was difficult to see exactly what was going on, but the end result was intriguing.

Trellis is often the ideal medium for covering or disguising objects such as boiler flues, aerials or water tanks. Care is obviously needed near a flue, which can get dangerously hot. Ensure that the trellis continues a theme used elsewhere in the garden so that it does not draw attention to itself. A virtually invisible access door can be incorporated and climbers will complete the picture.

Colour is another important consideration with trellis, as it is with all garden accessories. At one time, only white or dark green were acceptable, but so many colours are now available that you can link the garden and interior colour schemes in numerous ways. While pale, bleached or dragged colours are in vogue, reds, yellows and oranges can be dramatic: used in the right place, with a festoon of climbers creating a restful colour break, they could provide the perfect splash or drama in a contemporary roof or balcony. Black is often thought of as an unlikely colour, but in fact it is extremely useful as it absorbs light and allows a view to pass through or beyond it. Black trellis can create a subtle counterpoint and look good with similarly painted overheads.

The features and furnishings that make up the incidentals of a composition are legion. Not only do they bring a composition to life, they also provide a personal signature, making the space uniquely and intimately yours.

Above Trellis should be coloured more often; just look what interior designers can do with it. This gives the opportunity to link it in with both the adjoining house and incidental planting.

Below By clipping the plants above and around the back of the seat, the sweeping lines of the seat are emphasized, bringing a rhythm that might be lost against more general planting.

Glossary

Aggregate The **gravel** component of concrete which varies in size and can be exposed by brushing the concrete when nearly dry to produce a textured finish

Annuals Plants that complete their entire life-cycle within one growing season

Aphids Plant pests such as greenfly and blackfly

Bark chippings Used to provide a soft, textured surface over pathways and beds. They also act as **mulch** and exclude weed growth

Bituminous sealer Asphalt

Cleat A piece of wood or iron bolted onto the roof or wall onto which decking is attached to stop it slipping

Cobbles Rounded, kidney-shaped beach or river-bed pebbles, either used loose or bedded in **mortar** to form a textured surface

Coir A growing medium made from coconut husks

Coping The top course of masonry in a wall. This is usually more weatherproof than the rest of the wall and can be decorative

Crocks Broken pieces of pot used to cover the hole at the base of a pot to provide drainage without allowing the soil to be washed out

Damp proof course (DPC) A layer of moisture repellant material in a wall (usually) near the ground, to keep water from permeating the building

Deadhead To remove a wilting or faded flower from a plant without allowing its fruit or seed to mature

Ericacious compost Compost which is acidic in nature and therefore suitable for acid-loving plants such as heathers, azaleas and rhododendrons

Faience A cream-coloured form of **terracotta**

Fastigiate With a conical or tapering outline

Fibreglass Material made of a lightweight plastic containing strengthening fibrous strands of glass

Friable Easily crumbled, especially when dry

Granite setts Blocks, usually the size and shape of bricks, used for 'cobbling' roads in the nineteenth century and for contemporary paving

Gravel Broken stone or small dredged pebbles used as a loose textured surface or as **aggregate** in concrete

Ground-cover Low-growing plants that spread out and knit together. Useful as a form of weed prevention

Hardy Describes a plant that will usually survive winter out of doors in a given climate

Hoggin A mix of clay and **gravel** used as a 'binder' in gravel paths and drives

Ledger rail A horizontal **timber** rail bolted onto the face of a wall to provide support for decking

Lumber *see* **timber**

Mastic adhesive A **bituminous** flexible sealer

Mortar A smooth mixture of cement, sand, water and plasticizer for joining or bedding stones or bricks

Mulch A soil covering which retains moisture, reduces erosion and prevents weeds. Organic mulches, such as grass cuttings, enrich the soil

Perennials Plants that should live under usual circumstances for at least three growing seasons

Pergola Arbour or covered walk, usually with climbing plants trained over it

pH The measure of acidity or alkalinity: soil above pH7 is alkaline, that below pH7 is acid

Plywood Strong, thin board made by gluing together layers of wood with the grains at right angles

Repointing Repairing the damaged **mortar** between bricks on a wall or chimney

Shrubs Woody-stemmed plants, smaller than trees and usually divided into separate stems near the ground

Terracotta Unglazed, brownish-red, fine pottery

Timber (lumber) Wood prepared for building by being weathered and treated with preservative

Top dressing Replenishing the upper layers of soil to provide nutrients for plants

Topsoil The fertile upper layer of soil

Trellis Wooden lattice work attached to a wall or fence, or sometimes standing alone, up which climbing plants can be trained. Decorative or painted trellis can be a feature in its own right

Trompe-l'oeil A painting or decoration designed to give an illusion of reality

Veranda A low, raised deck around a house, usually shaded by the roof being extended over it

Vermiculite Lightweight, water-absorbent granules used as a potting medium

Index

Photographic acknowledgments

All photos by Jerry Harpur, with grateful thanks to the following garden owners, designers and architects:
B = bottom, C = centre, L = left, R = right, T = top

DESIGNER R. David Adams, Seattle 52T, 67, 147T: Art Centre, Hong Kong 31T: DESIGNER: Daniel Bainuel, Marrakech 18B: DESIGNER Michael Balston 155T: DESIGNER Michael Balston & Arabella Lennox-Boyd 41 (Little Malvern Court, Worcs), 117B, 147B: DESIGNERS Martina Barzi & Josefina Casares, Buenos Aires 8B, 29, 47B, 80, 86T, 125B, 148T: DESIGNER Barbara Britton, NYC 22B: DESIGNER Robert Broekema, Amsterdam 37B, 103B: DESIGNER Tim Callis, Cape Cod 130T: Carillon Point, Seattle 131: DESIGNERS Tom Carruth & John Furman, LA 45, 81: DESIGNERS Ted Chaffers & Dennis Lochen, Jesus Pobre, Spain 132L: DESIGNER Robert W. Chittock, Seattle 155B: DESIGNER Brian Coleman, Seattle 5, 49: DESIGNER Belt Collins, Hong Kong Ltd. 21T, 138B: DESIGNER Codie Conigliaro back jkt C: DESIGNER Keith Corlett, NYC 72, 92: DESIGNER Stephen Crisp, London 12B, 31B, 36, 40BL, 55B: DESIGNER Davis Dalbok, Living Green, SF 100B,136 137: DESIGNER Grover Dear, Archasia, Hong Kong 43T, 60L, 70B: DESIGNERS Delaney & Cochran, San Francisco 32B (for Bank of America), 39B, 66B, 140B: DESIGNER Norbert Deppisch, Ranatur, Munich 134B: DESIGNER Tim Du Val, New York 21B, 33 (copyright Conran Octopus Ltd), 37T, 43B, 57B, 74T, 87, 101, 104B, 141B: DESIGNER Laurie Eichengreen, NYC 38: DESIGNER Cristina Erhartdel, Buenos Aires back jkt T, back jkt B, 10–11, 20T, 74B: ARCHITECT Arthur Erickson, Vancouver 9, 42R: DESIGNER George Freedman, Sydney 20B, 79L, 151 (for the Bank of New South Wales) : Palacio Ca Sa Galesa, Palma de Mallorca 109: DESIGNER Edwina von Gal, New York 144B: DESIGNER Sonny Garcia, San Francisco 23, 82, 112, 114B, 128B, 148B, 149: Generalife, Alhambra Palace, Granada 95: DESIGNER Val Gerry, NYC 115: DESIGNER Isobelle C. Greene, Santa Barbara 35T, 83, 91, 103T, 110BL: Greenwood, Sydney 118T: Xavier Guerrand-Hermes, Marrakech 48T, 52B: DESIGNER Paul Guerin, London 71, 90T, 146: DESIGNER Perry Guillot, NYC 34T: DESIGNERS Perry Guillot & Iris Kaplow, NYC 34B: DESIGNER Arnout ter Haar, Amsterdam 55T: DESIGNER Raymond Hudson, Johannesburg 98, 125T: DESIGNER Iris Kaplow, NYC 93, 11: DESIGNER Galen Lee, NYC 2–3: DESIGNER Mel Light, LA 70T, 154:

DESIGNER Leif Ljungstrom, Palma de Mallorca 46, 48B: DESIGNER Michael Love, Sydney 19: DESIGNER Mallory Kirk Marshall, Dark Harbor, Maine 8T: DESIGNER Christopher Masson, London 94T, 110BR, 153: DESIGNER Jim Matsuo, Santa Monica 57T: DESIGNER/ARCHITECT Rick Mather, London 63: DESIGNER/CERAMICIST: Keeyla Meadows, Berkeley, CA 26B, 117T, 129: DESIGNER Jeff Mendoza, NYC 25, 39T, 68T, 90B, 99, 107T, 122B: Fred Mengoni, NYC 1: ARCHITECT Urbis Travers Morgan, Hong Kong 62B: DESIGNER Camille Muller, Paris, 123 (a terrace in NYC): DESIGNERS Chapin & Cynthia Nolen, Montecito, CA 76B: DESIGNER Cynthia Nolen, Montecito, CA 18T: 'Ohinetahi', Christchurch, NZ 4, 27: DESIGNERS Marijke van Oordt & Robert Tjebbes, Amsterdam 134T: DESIGNER William J. Overholt, Seattle 68B: DESIGNER Henrietta Parsons, London 97B: DESIGNERS Andrew Pfeiffer & Leslie J. Walford, Sydney 142: DESIGNER Patrick Presto, San Francisco 40B, R: DESIGNER Mark Rios, LA 84: DESIGNER Chris Rosmini, LA 133: DESIGNER Mark Rumary, Yoxford, Suffolk 59: DESIGNER Antonella Daroda Sartogo, Rome 6T, 32T, 54, 86B, 132R, 144T: La Casella, Alpes Maritimes: DESIGNERS Claus Scheinert & Thomas Parr 30T, 53: DESIGNER John Sewell, London 94B, 108: DESIGNERS Lon Shapiro & Sonny Garcia, San Francisco 138T: DESIGNER Roberta Sherman, Seattle 6B,113T, 119: DESIGNER Mary Riley-Smith, NYC 97T: DESIGNERS Leslie Smith & Eric Eichenboom, Cape Town 120 121, 152B: Mirabel Osler/DESIGNER Joe Smith, Dumfries 141T: Stellenberg, Cape Town 102, 107B: DESIGNER Rob Sterk, Amsterdam 88–89: DESIGNERS Barbara Stock & Stacey Hill, Seattle 14B, 24, 47T, 62B, 64, 100T, 122T: DESIGNER Stephen Suzman, San Francisco 35B, 73, 114T: Charlotte Temple, San Francisco 42L: Angela Theriot, San Francisco 50–51: ARCHITECT/DESIGNER Robert Tjebbes, Amsterdam 66T, 69T, 69C, 69B: Edmundo Tonconogy, Buenos Aires 30B: DESIGNER Jonathan Turner, London front jkt, 13, 14T, 143: Valdemossa, Majorca 140T: DESIGNER David J. Walsh, NYC 139: DESIGNER Donald J. Walsh, NYC 17, 145: Westbury Court 130B: DESIGNER John Wheatman, San Francisco 26T, 58, 118B: DESIGNER Anne Scott Wilkes, Sydney 96, 116: DESIGNER Albert Williams 113B: DESIGNER Robin Williams, Hungerford 15: Yacout Restaurant, Marrakech 150: DESIGNER Nadine Zamichow, NYC 105.